THE HERALD
DIARY

THE HERALD DIARY

That's the Sealiest Thing I've Read

Ken Smith

BLACK & WHITE PUBLISHING

First published 2016
by Black & White Publishing Ltd
29 Ocean Drive, Edinburgh EH6 6JL

1 3 5 7 9 10 8 6 4 2   16 17 18 19

ISBN: 978 1 78530 064 6

A CIP catalogue record for this book is available from the British Library.

Typeset by Iolaire Typesetting, Newtonmore
Printed and bound by CPI Group (UK) Ltd, Croydon, CR0 4YY

Contents

Introduction

You need a laugh after what has gone on in the past year. Fortunately readers of *The Herald* were up for it.

No matter the issue, whether it be Scottish independence, the European referendum, football, relationships, or even catching a bus, *Herald* readers found something funny amidst it all and told the newspaper's daily Diary column.

Here are the best of their stories, funny, wry and amusing whether you are a *Herald* reader or simply someone who likes to read about Scotland with a smile on their face.

1
Children

The days of giving a child a sandwich at the start of the school holidays and not seeing them again for a couple of months are over. Parents are now expected to entertain their children almost every waking moment. Here are their stories.

A READER was in a Glasgow diner where a father had ordered some cheese and biscuits for his young son. The lad looked dubiously at the array of cheeses and said: "Dad, I don't like cheese with holes in it!" Our reader applauds the father's inspired reply of: "Just eat the cheese and leave the holes at the side of the plate."

WE mentioned the school holidays, and a south side reader tells us she visited a friend the other day only to hear a huge commotion in the room upstairs. Her friend looked at the ceiling and explained: "I told the kids I was going to give all the toys they no longer played with to charity. That's them just now desperately playing with every toy they own."

AN INSPIRED answer in a Glasgow pub at the weekend when a toper chatting to his pals announced: "The wean's pet mouse Elvis died."

Immediately a pal asked: "Was he caught in a trap?"

WITH all the schools back, teachers are of course working hard. But as Duncan Johnston in Oban recalls: "My wife was a primary teacher in the days when salaries arrived as cheques in envelopes which were delivered round the classrooms. One day a boy asked what was in the envelope and my wife replied, 'That's my pay.' The boy asked, 'Where do you work?'"

FOR Hallowe'en a Newton Mearns reader tells us she had prepared little plastic pumpkins filled with sweets and fruit to hand out to the kids who came to the door. All the children took them and said thank you, apart from one little tot who raked through the pumpkin, pulled out a tangerine, handed it back to our reader and said: "I'll not be needing this."

WE always remember the Saltcoats reader who told us of the young lad coming to his door and proclaiming: "Trick or Treat? And by the way, mister, I'm diabetic, so it's cash only."

AND our favourite daft Hallowe'en gag. "Doctor, doctor - I keep making people think I'm about to tell them a joke."

A READER phones and asks: "Do you know what's fun?" He then explained: "Next time someone tells you the name of their new baby, repeat it back to them with their surname and innocently ask, 'Like the mass murderer?'"

A CROY reader heard two women on the train into Glasgow discussing the difficulties of renting properties with one declaring: "I get the impression that landlords who don't allow dogs, but do allow children, don't know very much about children."

A GROUP of women were discussing the games they play with their children when Amy Dillon confided: "My favourite game with the kids is one where I play dead until they go around to their dad's side of the bed and wake him up."

FOR sheer daftness, a Bearsden reader swears to us that a young lad got on his bus into Glasgow at Maryhill and was heard telling his pal: "I used to love sitting in supermarket trolleys when I was younger.

"But then my maw spoiled it by shouting over at me to get out of the canal."

MANY are the difficulties of having teenage children. A Lenzie reader emails to tell us: "My children sure do make a lot of plans for people who are unable to drive themselves anywhere."

A MILNGAVIE reader was picking up his granddaughter from nursery and was surprised she said she was hungry, as she had taken a sandwich and cream cake with her that morning. But she told him: "Kevin said they were poisoned - and I was not to eat them."

"So what happened to them?" asked her surprised granddad. "Kevin ate them. I hope he doesn't die!"

HAVE you seen these colouring books for adults which are a big seller these days? A West End reader tells us he was in his local cafe where a woman was colouring in such a book while her young son was running about, shrieking. Eventually as he ran past her she clipped his backside with the colouring book, and he stopped. She then told everyone in the cafe: "So it's true. These books do relieve stress."

A VIGNETTE on the pessimism of Glaswegians passed on by Michael Gray who says: "I heard a dad say to his wee girl in a Glasgow supermarket, 'Enjoy sitting in the trolley seat while you can. It doesn't last forever.' Wise words."

OUR story about the difficulties of having teenage children brings forth from a Clarkston reader: "If my kids knew there was a light in the oven, they'd leave that one on too."

A PAISLEY reader was in the Braehead shopping centre where he watched a harassed mother dealing with a gurning young boy who was constantly seeking her attention. Eventually she snapped at him: "Go and play with your wee brother. That's what we had him for."

A GLASGOW mother tells us she heard her daughter in the kitchen asking: "Dad, can I have a Kit Kat for my snack at school?" "No," replied her husband. "Why not?" said her daughter. "Because I said so," replied hubby.

[5]

After a pause, daughter asked: "You've eaten them all, haven't you?"

WE can never get enough stories about cute little kids. A Bearsden mother tells us it was her birthday, and she jokingly said to her toddler son: "What did you get me for my birthday?" and was surprised when he answered: "A cake." When she asked him where it was he replied: "You haven't made it yet."

GRANDPARENTS of course are spending a lot of time on child-minding duties these days. An Edinburgh reader did not know whether to be angry or impressed when he picked up his grand-daughter from nursery and asked her what she had done that day.

"A biscuit would help me remember," was the reply.

PARENTING is always a tricky business. A reader hears a chap in a Glasgow pub explain: "I make my son's lunch for him before he goes off to school. Then the other day he comes home and complains that I don't put any wee notes in it like other parents do. So today I wrote him a lovely wee letter saying 'Sorry I ate your pudding'."

SUNNY weather this week. But this is what our teachers are up against. A reader in Rhu overheard a local stopping to chat to a family he knew, and saying to the youngster: "Weren't you at school today?" The girl's mother intervened however to declare: "Ach, it was far too nice a day to send her to school."

OUR tales on parenting skills bring forth this claim from a Lenzie reader: "I've now learned that the only way to get my young son to flush the toilet is for me to be showering when he uses it."

A GLASGOW reader hears a young girl, wise beyond her years, tell her pal: "You can hit anyone, as hard as you want on their back, as long as you yell 'Spider!' at the same time. I did it to my sister and she thanked me."

A SOUTH side reader catching the train into town watched a young woman with a baby gladly hand her little one over to a neighbour who came over to have a cuddle. After the neighbour got off the train, the young mum's pal turned to her and said: "You let people hold your baby? I don't even let people hold my phone."

A PARENTING tip from a Bearsden reader who informs us: "Beware if your child starts cleaning their room without being nagged into doing it. It only means they are about to ask you for an outrageous sum of money."

A NEWTON Mearns reader sends us a telephone message received by a friend from her mother who explains that she had to bring the girl's sister home from primary school early as she was very sad, and had a "very hard day". Mum went on to explain that the wee sister had taken her two pet snails to school, had taken them out her bag in class, and they were then thrown out the window by the classroom assistant who assumed they had somehow wandered in from outside.

Although the sister was now laughing heartily, her mum ended the message: "Please act sad about it when you get home."

A READER looking over his son's Modern Studies Higher paper was reminded of his own days at school when he had a project on the Second World War. He interviewed his own father, and as he tells us: "I reached the point where I felt I had to ask, in a somewhat quiet voice, whether he had ever killed anyone. My dad answered in an equally quiet voice, 'Probably. I was a cook for some time'."

OUR story about the dad being asked by his son if he killed anyone in the war reminds Ron Sretwell in East Kilbride of a picture in the house of himself in uniform when he did National Service in the 1950s.

His then young son looked at it and quietly asked: "Did you see much fighting?" Says Ron: "I told him, 'yes I did'. I just omitted to say that I was only at the Royal Artillery depot in Woolwich and the fighting was on a Friday night in the Welcome Inn, Woolwich."

AN AYRSHIRE reader was at his golf club where one of the regulars announced: "I told the wife that I wanted an agreement where I would see the kids every second weekend."

There was a pause before he added: "But she said that as we were still married and lived together I had to see them every day."

ENTERTAINING children during school holidays, a Glasgow reader tells us he kept his six-year-old amused with painting. Hours later the lad came into the room with his picture, demanding to know why it was in the kitchen bin. Dad is pleased with his quick-thinking reply: "It was too good. I didn't want your sisters to be jealous."

YES, the school holidays have begun. A reader in the Braehead shopping centre heard a father shout at his two squealing children who were running around and getting in everyone's way. Said the dad: "Stop that! Or I'll get mad."

However, the two youngsters ignored him and carried on with their racket. He then shouted: "Stop that or your mum'll get mad." Suddenly there is an immediate halt to the running around.

FATHER'S Day on Sunday was being discussed in a Glasgow pub yesterday where one toper told his friends: "Got my own back on Sunday. I ran into my boys' room at two in the morning and shouted, 'Can I open my Father's Day present yet?'"

2

The Glasgow Pub

The days of men spending most evenings in the pub on their way home have declined due to family pressures, a shortage of free time, and stricter drink driving laws. But there were still the occasional forays into licensed premises which were worth recording.

A READER hears a young chap entering a Glasgow pub to meet his pals announce that he had stopped off for a burger in a local fast food restaurant before joining them for a bevvy. He explained: "The guy behind the counter apologised for them running out of lettuce. I had to tell him, 'Trust me, no one comes in here for lettuce'."

A READER swears to us he heard a young woman on the bus into Glasgow ask her pal: "How drunk were you on Saturday? You were dancing like a woman trying to put on pants four sizes too small with a wasp flying round her head."

Dear Alcohol, we had a deal where you would make me funnier, smarter and a better dancer ...... I saw the video, we need to talk!

WE mentioned the vexed topic of Scottish notes being accepted or not accepted in England. A Motherwell fan tells us four of them were at a pre-season friendly in England where they ordered four pints.

Realising they were tendering a Scottish £20, they also asked for crisps.

When the barman turned to get the snacks they all took a gulp from their pints, assuming that their Scottish note would now be accepted without a fuss.

A READER phones to tell us that Glasgow's city centre can still be a colourful place. He says the girl in front of him in a taxi queue at the weekend told her pal: "Ah was mortified. Ah stood behind a guy thinking he was using a cash machine as ah wanted to take some money out. Turns out he was only leaning against a wall having a pee."

READER John Neil likes to play with stereotypes as he tells us: "Wild weather again here in Stornoway today. Think I just heard on the local radio that police are advising locals to go out only if they are desperate for a drink."

A TOPER in a Glasgow pub at the weekend was getting a bad time from his pals for drinking by himself at home. He tried to defend himself with: "You say 'drinking alone'. I prefer to call it 'preparing for unexpected company'."

SCATHING remark of the week that we heard in a Glasgow pub was the woman discussing a mutual acquaintance who told her pal: "I could tell by the scowl on her face that her patience, and her botox, were wearing thin."

A READER hears a chap in a Glasgow pub explain: "I woke up suddenly with a jolt and my first thought was that I was going to be late for work.

"But then I realised I was at work, so I was able to relax."

A READER hears a Glasgow pub conversation where a toper declared: "I hate these motorway service vehicles with stripes on the back. I slowed down for one thinking it was a police car."

"So basically," replied his pal: "You're complaining about being tricked into obeying the law for no reason?"

A READER tells us he was in a Glasgow pub at the weekend when he heard a young lad tell his pals: "My New Year's resolution was not to have any sex this year.

"Apparently."

AND we think it's the weather that's making everyone so pessimistic. A reader swears to us he heard a chap in a bar in Glasgow at the weekend tell his pals: "I wish I could just go back to the good old day." Naturally one of his pals asked: "Don't you mean good old days?" But the chap merely replied: "No, I just had the one."

A READER tells us he was in a smart Glasgow hostelry the other night when an attractive woman, perhaps a little unsteady, weaved past him to the loo. On her return she stopped and squeezed his thigh to get his attention. "You don't by any chance," she whispered, "know where I was sitting, as I've forgotten who I came here with."

YOU don't hear much about karaoke these days. John Sword was recalling when karaoke bars first began in Glasgow and his pal went up to sing. When he returned to his table his wife merely told him: "The singer before you must have really been rotten. They were still booing him all the way through your song."

A YOUNG chap in a Glasgow pub at the weekend was weaving a tale for his pals about being stopped by the police while driving. He claimed: "I got a bit flustered when one of them asked how fast I was going. I told them that I had moved in with my girlfriend after we'd only been going out for three months. Apparently that's not what they meant."

THE Saracen's Head pub near Glasgow's Barras often attracts tourists as it is one of Glasgow's oldest pubs - although it lacks the sophistication of establishments in the city centre. John Mulholland tells us: "I paid my first visit to the legendary Saracen's Head last Saturday. It was empty. A well-to-do couple arrived and the lady asked if they served Irish Coffee. 'Aye, nae problem,' said the barman. 'How many spoonfuls of Nescafé dae ye take? Milk or nae milk?' With no mention of cream, I felt this was going to be a tricky situation. But, fair play to the woman, she confirmed her order and then told the barman that his mug of coffee with a quarter gill of whisky in it was the best she'd had."

WE'VE all been there. As comedy writer Brian Limond explains: "I was in a pub and tried to pour myself another cup of tea from the teapot. But it was finished. So I looked like I was having an imaginary tea party."

A READER was in Glasgow's Griffin Bar in Glasgow when a chap came in and asked if he could book the function room at short notice. The barmaid looked at the book and said she was sorry, but there was a comedy night arranged for that evening. The unhappy chap blurted out: "Aww, yer havin' a laugh." The barmaid couldn't help replying: "Hope so."

A READER hears a bar-room philosopher in Glasgow opine: "With me, it's not pride that comes before a fall. It's a night out on vodka and a coffee table that I forgot existed."

BOBSIE Mullen, mine host at the Griffin Bar opposite Glasgow's King's Theatre, likes to put jokey messages on the blackboard outside. So when the BBC reported that a glossy ibis had flown from Africa to make a rare appearance in Scotland, Bobsie wrote on the board: "GLOSSY IBIS welcome. No crapping on the floor though!" Days later he received a registered letter from an irate pensioner who wrote: "Your sign welcoming IBS customers as long as they do not make a mess on the floor is insulting. I enclose a book about irritable bowel syndrome to enlighten you on what thousands of us have to suffer."

Bobsie says the sender did not sign it so he is unable to reply, suggesting an eye test.

BEAUTIFUL ONE OFF 18 CARROT GOLD PLATED CHAIN Real fresh

3
Reaching for the Stars

Scots love seeing star performers - but don't always treat them with the respect that the stars foolishly believe they deserve. Here are some of the tales from our theatres and cinemas.

WE mentioned the flak Andrew Lloyd Webber received for flying in from New York to back the government on cutting tax credits to the poor. *Rab C Nesbitt* author Ian Pattison reminds us: "Years ago at the Glasgow premiere of Lloyd Webber's *Cats* at the King's Theatre, Cameron Mackintosh, the producer, was in attendance. One of the guests was Jack Milroy, the sunnier half of Francie and Josie. At the interval Mackintosh stopped Milroy and asked, 'How are you enjoying *Cats*?' Jack replied, 'It's no' bad, son. But it could do with a wee dug running aboot to liven it up a bit'."

THE second series of the Scottish-based historical romp Outlander is launched next month. An actor who worked on it tells us that filming in Scotland's worst weather was harsh. He went on: "At one point the director ordered a few of us dressed as Highlanders to take a couple of horses and be silhouetted on a hill in the driving rain while they filmed. After a while we saw a couple of helpers struggling up the hill carrying blankets.

"That cheered us up - until they finally arrived and put them over the horses."

GOOD to see singer Adele is still as down to earth as ever. Appearing at Glasgow's Hydro at the weekend she looked at the giant screen behind her showing a huge close-up of her face, and told the audience: "Thank God I've not got a cold sore."

WE ASKED for your Glasgow Empire stories after David Hayman announced he was holding a charity Empire nostalgia night at the Citizens Theatre for Spirit Aid and the Clutha Trust, and reader Sandy Thomson in Cromarty reminds us of the great tale of Dorothy Squires: "When she appeared as a support act at the Empire near the end of her career, the audience - impatiently waiting for the main act - greeted her appearance with jeers and catcalls. In a brief moment of silence, however, a lone voice from the balcony yelled: 'Shut up and let the auld bag sing.' Miss Squires's response? 'Well I'm glad to see there is one gentleman in the audience.'"

JOHN Gracie, the legendary trumpeter who has just retired from the Royal Scottish National Orchestra after 35 years, was a favourite with composers, including Elmer Bernstein of *The Magnificent Seven* fame and Jerry Goldsmith who wrote *Star Trek* music.

John tells the story that he once phoned fellow trumpeter and friend Maurice Murphy of the London Symphony Orchestra and asked how he was getting on.

"Oh, alright John," he replied. "We're recording the music for a film with a big bear in it." The film was *Star Wars*.

ACTRESS and comedienne Dorothy Paul is coming out of retirement to appear at the That's Fife comedy festival this April. We remember her colourful description of the early days when work wasn't plentiful. "I was so desperate I was eating the grapes off the wallpaper," said Dorothy.

SHOUTING out at concerts, continued. A reader in Rhu tells us: "For several years there was a guy who seemed to appear at every rock concert in the city. His claim to fame? During every show he would wait until there was a quiet passage of music or a hush between songs before bawling out, 'Hallo! Ahm oan yer bootleg!'"

More sotto voce was George Tomlinson's girlfriend when they attended a concert at Glasgow's Woodside Halls given by famous sitar player Ravi Shankar. Says George: "Ravi was into his second or third morning raga, the tonal framework for composition and improvisation, when my girlfriend whispered to me, 'Has he tuned up yet?'"

"PHIL Collins is getting a lot of mentions on social media," said the chap in Glasgow. "Has he died?" asked his pal. "Worse than that," he replied. "He says he's coming out of retirement."

THAT great Scottish play exposing the worst excesses of capitalism in Scotland, *The Cheviot, the Stag, and the Black, Black Oil* was revived by Dundee Repertory Theatre after a gap of nearly a quarter of a century. We did worry that it was being forgotten about a few years ago when Edinburgh Filmhouse put out a press release saying their season of films celebrating Highland culture would include *The Cheviot, the Stag, and the Black, Black Olive.*

OUR stories of Glasgow's dance halls remind a reader of the classic tale of the chap trying to smuggle a half bottle under his jacket into the dancing, but just as he approached the door, the bottle slipped and smashed on the pavement. With the door-man moving menacingly towards him, the chap looks up at the windows above the door and shouts: "Hey you! That could've killed somebody."

STRICTLY Come Dancing returns to the telly. We like the slow dawning of realisation of competitor Jeremy Vine, who told the Radio Times on his first meeting with the rest of the dancers: "As I gazed around, the thing that worried me was: there was no buffoon. No idiot. Nobody who couldn't dance."

ACTOR Rupert Everett was in Glasgow for the Citizens Theatre's 70th birthday celebrations. Rupert, whose acting career began at the Gorbals theatre in the 1970s, once fondly recalled: "Provided the play ended at 10.20 when the last bus left, the audience really enjoyed themselves at the Citz. However, if the show ran on even a minute late, the audience would still get up at 10.20 - and you could hear the clatter, clatter, clatter of their seats as they left."

ON audience questions Jim Morrison tells us: "On a cruise a few years ago we had on board the actress Shirley Anne Field, who gave a talk of her life, and then asked if anyone had any questions. After a pause a large Scouse chap put his hand up,

'Have you ever had a facelift?' 'No', replied Shirley, 'But I can give you the address of a place that does them if you want'."

SINGER David Essex is returning to Glasgow's King's Theatre in November for his only Scottish date in his first major tour in four years.

We recall a previous visit to Glasgow by Essex when an adoring fan handed him a glow strip which he tried to fix around his wrist but was struggling with it. Another woman rushed forward to the stage and gestured for him to lower his wrist. As she worked away, he looked down and asked: "You're not trying to steal my watch are you?"

THE upmarket Four Seasons Restaurant in Manhattan is closing, and the *New York Times* Style section sent a reporter to photograph diners and ask them who designed their clothes. All pretty vapid stuff until that great old diplomat Henry Kissinger strolled out, and the conversation, as reported in the *NYT*, went: "May I ask you where your suit is from?" "My what?" "Where did you get your suit?" "I have no idea." "How was lunch?" "I think we've done enough." "OK. Thanks so much."

A COLLEAGUE wants to talk about the new Mary Poppins film. We have to hand it to him as he takes a deep breath and tells us faultlessly: "It's going to be a very dark film. The new *Mary Poppins* will feature a super-calloused fragile mystic hexed by halitosis."

TALKING of bad weather, it reminds John Bannerman of the rain that poured down at T in the Park this summer. He recalled: "My 16-year-old grandson and three pals were dropped someway far off from the venue, and were exhausted when they arrived at an open mud bath. An ancient East-of-Scotland spiv offered to carry their heavy luggage to their far-off tent site in his wheelbarrow, which they gladly accepted, at the extortionate cost of £40. After about 50 yards, the old codger feigned a dizzy spell, and they had to push the wheelbarrow themselves, and return it to him. No discount was offered to the young lads. He performed this trick several times afterwards."

OL' Blue Eyes himself, Frank Sinatra, would have been 100 years old last week if he had lived. We remember when Frank passed away and the newspaper vendor at Central Station was bawling out: "Frank Sinatra deid! Start spreading the news!"

TICKETS have gone on sale for Omid Djalili's show at the King's Theatre as part of this year's Glasgow International Comedy Festival.

We are sure it will be a far better show than the one reviewed years ago in The Herald when the reviewer stated: "Apparently the D in Djalili is silent - just as I was during his jokes."

MARCEL Lucont, the arrogant French bon vivant and alter ego of comedian Alexis Dubus, is appearing at Glasgow's Drygate. We remember when he appeared at the Edinburgh Fringe,

came on stage at the Gilded Balloon, pointed at a woman and declared in his mock French accent: "You! Give me a type of fruit." When the startled woman stuttered: "Apple" he replied: "Not verbally. I've been in this Scottish city for three weeks and it's almost impossible to find any fruit."

FRENCH designer Philippe Starck was being interviewed in the *London Standard* where he was asked what he collected. He said: "I dislike collecting, but when I buy shoes I buy 20 pairs so I can have them in all my houses, and when I buy a T-shirt I buy 80." Then: "What would you do as mayor for the day?" to which he replied: "Work on the difference between rich and poor. In

London the rich are really rich and the poor are really poor. It's not acceptable."

FAREWELL to music festival Celtic Connections in Glasgow after another great year. Mike Ritchie tells us: "Folk singer Bella Gaffney covered a song by the late John Martyn during her sparkling set at the Danny Kyle Open Stage Sunday session at Celtic Connections. She introduced it by saying, 'I've always wanted to be able to play the guitar like John Martyn - but I've only ended up so far drinking like him'."

ROD Stewart is returning to play two dates at Glasgow's Hydro in December after opening the concert hall in 2013. We remember that on a previous visit Rod stopped at one of his favourite pubs, the Wee Barrel in Paisley, en route to Glasgow Airport, and bought everyone inside a drink. Anyway, an old fellow in the corner raised his glass and called over: "Thanks son. Did you have a wee win on the horses?"

GOOD to see Jackie Kay named as the new national poet of Scotland, the Makar. We remember when a school pupil cheek-ily told her that her poems were coming up in his English Prelim and did she have any tips. Jackie told him: "A friend of mine, a poet, went to night classes to get his A-level English. On exam day his own poem came up and he failed!"
  We also liked her refreshingly honest reply when she wrote about her search for her biological father in *Red Dust Road*, and

an audience member asked her how difficult it had been to find him. "I put his name in Google and up popped pop," said Jackie.

GOODNESS. Now that's a lot of celebrities who have been squirrelling away their money abroad. We pass on the reaction of American entertainer Bette Midler, who remarked: "Did you hear about all the names released in the Panama Papers? Personally, my offshore financial plan is singing show tunes on cruise ships."

WE mentioned the collection of essays about the late Scottish Labour Minister Sam Galbraith, Remembering Sam being published by Birlinn. In it, his fellow MP Brian Wilson writes: "Sam was never overawed by celebrity or reputation. In fact, sometimes he didn't even recognise it. A journalist friend of mine, Duncan Campbell, was - and still is - in a relationship with the actress Julie Christie. One night not long after becoming MPs, a crowd of us went out for a meal and Sam was sitting opposite Julie. After a couple of convivial hours, there was a lull in the conversation and the unmistakable Galbraith tones rang out for all to hear, 'And what do you do yourself, Julia?'"

A FORMER colleague reminds us that Sam was one of the longest survivors in the world of a lung transplant. He tells us: "About a year or so after the transplant, I met Sam on the campaign trail and asked him how he was. 'Oh, better than the alternative,' he told me, and then with a typical Sam aside, he added, 'It just feels funny coughing up someone else's phlegm every morning'."

TALENTED Glasgow actress Siobhan Redmond is to star in Liz Lochhead's new play *Thon Man Molière* at Edinburgh's Royal Lyceum in May. We always liked Siobhan's reflections in *The Herald* about being interviewed when she said: "When I was coming into contact with journalists for the first time, I had nothing to say, I knew nothing, I knew nobody, I'd been nowhere.

"Gradually, I realised if only I had a hobby, I'd have something to talk about, so I sent away for a tapestry footstool kit, which I've still not unwrapped, because the longer I keep it unfinished, the longer I've got a hobby I can talk about."

BBC Scotland has announced a new series of the hit comedy *Still Game*, with Ford Kiernan and Greg Hemphill returning as Glasgow pensioners Jack Jarvis and Victor McDade nearly a decade after the last series. As one fan said on the delay: "Were you waiting until you didn't need make-up?"

WE mentioned Bob Dylan's concert in Glasgow 50 years ago this week, and reader Grant Young recalls: "I was reminded of the Dylan concert in the SECC in Glasgow a couple of years ago, when Bob was into offering new, rather arty, versions of many of his weel kent songs.

The fact that most of them were going right over the heads of many in the audience was illustrated after about half-an-hour, when, during a lull between two songs, a rather plaintive Glasgow voice inquired, 'Haw pal, do ye ken ony Bob Dylan songs'?"

ROY Gullane was watching the TV programme *Room 101* when a contestant said she wanted the film Bambi put in said room as it was too sad. Recalled Roy: "I was reminded of my own first viewing, at a very young age, of the Disney classic. The saddest scene, when a hunter kills Bambi's mother, leads to the very distraught child Bambi wandering through the forest calling, 'Mummy, mummy where are you?' In the midst of this heartbreak and anguish a voice boomed out from the bowels of the cinema, 'Am at the butcher's!' "No childhood Bambi trauma for me. Thank you Glasgow."

ACTOR Bert Kwouk, who played Cato in the *Pink Panther* films alongside Peter Sellers, has sadly died. Growing up in Shanghai he became a smoker, like most young men after the war. We liked an interview he gave when he explained: "When I did my first ever *Pink Panther* film, everybody smoked. Ten years later, when I got to *The Return Of The Pink Panther*, nobody smoked, except me. And Blake Edwards the director had given up smoking, and was very anti-smoking. So, from smoking on the set, I now had to creep around and find a quiet little corner somewhere, and have a quick puff.

"So I wasn't really looking for a place on set to jump out at

Peter, but was looking for a place to have a quick drag."

SHOUTING out at concerts, continued. Gerry MacKenzie goes behind the scenes as it were, and tells us: "In 1971 the King's Theatre in Glasgow was staging Wagner's Ring Cycle, and I was one of the stage crew. The cast was stellar and included world renowned bass David Ward from Dumbarton. During a performance the stage crew were nattering just a tad too loudly for David's liking. He ambled over and whispered, 'Sotto voce, for **** sake, guys'."

PERHAPS the most popular female comedian in America just now, Amy Schumer, is coming to the Edinburgh Playhouse at the end of August. We always liked her waspish statement: "All my friends are getting married. I guess I'm just at that age where people give up."

CONGRATULATIONS to Stones guitarist Ronnie Wood becoming a father of twins at the age of 68. We always remember his memorable quote when he was once asked about the legendary thriftiness of his old mate Rod Stewart. "Rod," said Ronnie, "is tighter than two coats of paint."

CINEMA shouts continued. Says Alex Skivington in Jordanhill: "I remember watching a cowboy film in the old Tivoli cinema in Patrick when there was a scene where a naked girl was washing herself behind a really dirty window.

"Everyone was peering in silence, trying to make out any details they could of the woman, when a shout came out from the back, 'Anyone got a shammy?'"

IT is comedy legend Stanley Baxter's 90th birthday this week. We only recently flicked through a volume of his *Parliamo Glasgow* sketches, which are still funny after all those years. The premise is that a retired Oxbridge anthropology professor visits Glasgow, and one of his stories is: "I requested directions and a small patriarchal gentleman came to my assistance. 'Centrul Station,' he intoned. Then to my amazement, he commenced to conjugate one of the lesser-known Latin verbs, 'Gerrabus, norisbus, anurrabus, heerabus!' Brilliant".

STAND-UP Bennett Arron, a regular at the Stand comedy club in Glasgow, also does a number of corporate gigs for companies around the UK that can be quite lucrative for comedians. He tells us however: "The weirdest feedback I received from a corporate gig was, 'Thanks for hosting our awards. You were funnier than we expected'. There is nothing like having low expectations."

CONGRATULATIONS on Rod Stewart receiving a knighthood. We remember James Mortimer explaining that when he opened Victoria's nightclub in Glasgow years ago, it did little business in its first month, leading to nervous bank managers phoning him daily. Then after a Scotland game Rod Stewart arrived in a Scotland top, sang with the customers, and was eventually poured into a taxi by two barmaids.

Two days later customers were queuing round the block. James explained: "Folk thought that Victoria's was too posh for them, but then they reckoned, 'Well if Rod can get drunk there so can we'."

MIKE Ritchie spots an interview with Edinburgh singer/songwriter Fraser Anderson, who has a new album, *Under The Cover of Lightness*, in which he was asked: "What is the best part of being a singer/song writer?" We can't help thinking it was a particular Scottish response when Fraser replied: "I can drink before lunch in my local bar and not be judged for it."

THIS week's big star at Glasgow's Hydro was veteran American crooner Barry Manilow.

Great show apparently. He's had a few bits of face surgery over the years which is why one fan declared: "Plastic - but still magic!" Anyway, fellow fan Fi Gilmore reminisced after the Glasgow show: "Twenty years ago I went travelling around the world. Tonight I am seeing Barry Manilow.

"Think the tickets cost the same."

WE never knowingly turn down a Chic Murray story so after our story about buying a train ticket, Ian Barnett reminds us: "Chic once told the story of being at Glasgow Central station and asking at the ticket office, 'Single to London'. The ticket seller, trying to be helpful, told Chic, 'Change at Preston'. Chic immediately replied, 'No thanks - I'll take my change now'."

AUDIENCE interventions were not just at the cinema. George Wishart in Borgue, Dumfries and Galloway, tells us: "After the St Andrew's Hall burned down in Glasgow, an old cinema in Anderston became a concert hall. A modern jazz quartet was playing there when a punter, holding a rolled-up raincoat, staggered down to the front of the balcony and shouted: "Play us a song we know Jimmy." He dropped his raincoat and it opened like a parachute as it descended on to the stalls.

"The punter was last seen staggering down to retrieve it as the band played."

OUR mention of the late great Scots comedian Chic Murray reminds fellow entertainer Andy Cameron of travelling with Chic to Aberdeen to record a TV show with Grampian Television.

Says Andy: "We stopped for a cup of tea in Laurencekirk and the lady who owned the tea room was obviously a fan of my radio show. As she placed the bill on the table Chic picked it up and declared, 'Excuse me dear, you can't expect Scotland's top entertainer to pay for his tea ... Andy will get it' and he handed me the bill."

THEATRICAL shouts continued. Says a reader: "Many years ago my wife and I went to the Val Doonican summer show in

Great Yarmouth. A comedian came on and bombed completely. Every joke was treated with silence. In an act of desperation he knelt down and prayed into the microphone, 'Oh lord what do I need to do to make them laugh?' The silence was broken by a Glasgow voice shouting, 'Say something funny ya tube'. Cue the early appearance of Val to rescue him."

SHOUTING out at the cinema, continued. Says John Crawford in Lytham: "In the late 50s many a good horror film in the George Cinema, Kilbirnie, was spoiled when the hero was about to lift the lid on Dracula's coffin, only for somebody to shout out, 'Take the money' then somebody else would shout, 'Naw, open the box' in the vernacular of a TV Quiz show that was very popular at the time."

WE read on the BBC news site that an Edinburgh University worker tried to defraud the uni out of £14,000 by submitting a fictitious invoice for taxidermy services. For some reason it reminds us of the chap who took two stuffed dogs to an Antiques Roadshow episode. When the presenter told him: "This is a very rare breed, have you any idea what they would fetch if they were in good condition?" The chap replied: "Sticks."

CINEMA shouts continued. Says Linda FitzGerald in Killin: "The old King's Picture House in Greenock was rumoured to be haunted so your nerves were on edge before you were seated. Dracula, in the film Dracula in the 1970s, with bats flying around him, was in the graveyard, about to drink the beautiful girl's blood, when suddenly there was a bat actually in the cinema building. It was flitting around, attracted to the projector light. A guy in the balcony jumped up grabbing at his own throat and screamed, 'Oh my neck!' This was followed by a mass exodus of the frantic hysterical audience trying to get out the doors."

ALEX Macintyre remembers attending a talent contest in Douglas, Isle of Man. A budding Elvis Presley was struggling manfully through Wooden Heart, and when he reached the line 'But I don't have a wooden heart' a Glasgow voice was heard to shout out 'You maybe haven't got a wooden heart but you've got a brass neck!'

ACTOR Sir Roger Moore is coming to Glasgow's Theatre Royal in November to have a chat about his career. We remember when Roger was interviewed by Scottish journalist Alan Fisher for GMTV in Kosovo, where the actor was invited in his role as an ambassador for Unicef. Said Alan: "Killing time before our live cross to London I didn't want to do the obvious thing and ask him about Bond, so, remembering a trailer I saw, I asked if The Spice Girls movie was the last thing he'd done.

"He gave me a smile, raised his eyebrow, and answered in that wonderful voice, 'Yes'. After a dramatic pause, he added: 'And it was sh***!'"

Roger once told the story that actor Noel Coward was asked

to play the villain in the Bond film *Dr No*. He sent the producers a telegram that simply stated: "Dr No? No! No! No!"

SANJEEV Kohli says he loves the all-female *Ghostbusters* film. "I just hope they don't remake it with an all-male cast and ruin it."

CINEMA shouts continued. Says Norma Gibb: "When *The Exorcist* was the scariest film to see, I went with my pals to The Strand in Alexandria. Just as we were having palpitations, looking at the grotesque vision of the lassie "possessed" by the devil, with peelywally cracked skin, red bulging eyes, copiously spewing green gunge, and her head turning 360 degrees, a voice shouted down from the balcony, 'Well, hullo therrr, doll'. A comedian or a chancer - I'll never know."

ANDY Cameron recalls: "There were 25,000 people at Celtic Park to see Rod Stewart do a show. In the middle of Maggie May, Rod told them, "Come on, Glasgow I think you know this one" and a wee Glasgow punter shouted out: "Aye, we dae know it Rod but at 75 quid a ticket we thought you might sing it."

CINEMA shouts continued. Jim Adamson from Greenock remembers a night at the BB Cinema when a character opined he loved the feel of a pear. A voice from the back stalls cried, "A pair of whit?"

We had also mentioned a screening of *The Exorcist* and it

reminds Roy Gullane: "Many years ago I went to a matinee performance of *The Exorcist*. There I was, in the cinema surrounded
by OAPs, watching the young Linda Blair lying in her bed, head
spinning, covered in green slime. Scary? Briefly, until I heard the
old lady behind me, obviously one of those real Glasgow wifies
that had seen everything say, 'Aw, the wee sowl!'"

WE end our cinema shouts with Jim Currie in Lenzie recalling:
"I saw the film *The Brothers* in The State cinema in Shettleston
where the big star was Patricia Roc.

"In a torrid love scene all you could see was her fist clenching
and slowly unclenching. Inevitably a voice shouted, 'Move the
picture over a bit!'"

4

Raising Teenagers

Raising teenagers can be deeply rewarding - but can also be deeply challenging. Our readers confided their funniest moments with their offspring as they moved into becoming young adults.

WELL that's most of the Highers finished at Scottish schools, and the poor things have just got to wait for the results now to find out if they are getting into the university of their choice. It reminds us of the tale of the university graduation in Scotland where a reader swears to us he saw a sobbing grandmother hold on to her graduating grandson and tell him: "Your parents would have been so proud seeing you up on that stage today." After giving him another squeeze she added: "It's a shame they couldn't be bothered to come."

"I SWEAR," said the middle-aged man on the train from Bearsden into Glasgow, "that if my daughter was stranded on a desert island she would spell out the message on the beach with big stones, 'What's the Wi-Fi password?'"

A READER hears a student on Glasgow's Byres Road complain: "When I was really young I couldn't wait to grow up and make my own decisions," before adding: "What made me think that would be fun?"

A READER in Botanic Gardens at the weekend passes on a conversation he heard amongst some student-types who were discussing fishing, and how stupid fish were. Finally one student argued: "They don't seem that stupid to me. If a pie dropped out of the sky and just hung there above my head, I'd take a bite at it."

RAISING teenagers, continued. A reader emails: "My daughter asked me what it was like when I was her age. So I took all her electronics away and made her play with a Rubik's Cube. She wasn't happy."

ON THAT point parents, are you looking forward to teenage kids lolling around the house for the next couple of months? A reader swears to us that his teenage daughter shouted down to him: "Dad, what's the new Wi-Fi password?" He shouted back: "You can have it once you've tidied your room." There was a pause for a minute or two before she replied: "Still not working. Is that all lower case?"

DEALING with teenagers continued. A Pollokshields reader confesses that when her daughter announced her room was clean, she couldn't help but tell the young one: "You keep using that word. You should know that it doesn't mean what you think it means."

A HERALD reader in Whitecraigs fears his son's aspirations are too limited.

The lad, who has just finished yoonie, and still kicking about at home, was asked by a neighbour: "What are you doing after you graduate?" and his son replied: "I think my folks are going to take me out for a meal."

LIPPY teenagers continued. A reader on the south side said that as it had turned a little chilly he searched for a favourite garment, and eventually shouted out to the household: "Have you seen my denim jacket?" His teenage daughter shouted back: "I've just checked. It's not going to be the 80s today."

OUR story about the difficulties of getting teenagers to tidy their rooms reminds a Bishopbriggs reader: "I was always amazed how my daughter, rather than empty the bin in her bedroom, would carefully add items to it like she was building a giant Jenga puzzle."

A READER phones to ask us: "Why is it I would have to own a car for at least 30 years before it would be described as vintage, yet my daughter says that the phone I bought her only six months ago is vintage, and needs replaced."

WE mentioned students going back to university, and a West End reader who studied theology tells us when he was at uni folk kept on asking him why he had chosen the subject. He eventually took to giving the reply: "God knows why", which seemed to keep everyone happy.

TALKING of students, we hear from one who tells us: "I woke up, and when stretching out, found a pound coin under my pillow. You've no idea the feeling of panic I had - until I checked all my teeth were still in place."

WRITER Deedee Cuddihy tells us: "It's good to see that work produced by art students still has the ability to confuse and confound.

"At the Tontine Building in Glasgow, where part of the Glasgow School of Art degree show is being held, one perplexed visitor, having viewed such works as a pile of rotting bananas and a cake made with the artist's own pee, wrote in the comments book, 'Ah dinny get ony oh it'."

A PARTICK reader strolls past new student accommodation in the West End and reads on the sales banner outside that it included: "On-site cinema, private gym, study rooms and dinner party room."

He tells us: "I am unsure whether I am more offended by the notion of modern-day students having a room in which to study or a room in which to throw dinner parties. In my time at uni I didn't do either."

EVEN students are now returning to university after the Christmas/New Year break. A Hyndland reader said he heard one student in Byres Road tell his pals: "I think I'm going to email the makers of frozen meals to explain to them that no-one actually knows the wattage of their microwaves."

5
Law

━━━━━━━━━

Not funny being arrested, but our police officers and lawyers do try to lighten the gloom with the occasional funny.

GREAT the advice you can receive from the cops on-line these days. Dumfries and Galloway Police put on social media yesterday: "Contacted on social media from a female who's suggesting you both take your clothes off? It's a scam. They film you and demand money. Be aware."

Thanks for that. It reminds us of the gag about the chap warning his pals about a woman who distracts you in a car park by taking her top off while her pal pickpockets you. He said it had happened to him three times that week.

"DID you see that *The X Factor* judge Simon Cowell's house was broken into?" said the toper in a Glasgow pub at the weekend. "Bet his CD collection was untouched," replied his pal.

DEEDEE Cuddihy's latest pocket-sized book, *The Wee Guide to Scottish Women: The Good, the Bad and the Gallus*, out soon. One bloke relates how a slim, blonde young woman, her hair in a ponytail, came into his shop. "She was quite attractive but the main reason I noticed her was that she only had one leg and was on crutches," he says. "After a short while, it became apparent that she had come in to shoplift so she was escorted off the premises and told not to come back." A few days later, the woman re-appeared. When she was reminded that she had been barred, she said: "You must have me mixed up with someone else."

SAD to hear of the death of legendary Glasgow Sheriff J Irvine Smith, who had a great love of the English language. He once told a felon, when finding him guilty, that he was a "fecund liar". The chap's solicitor told Irvine afterwards that his client had remarked it was the first time in his criminal career he had heard the bench using language which he could readily understand.

He was also a great after-dinner speaker and once introduced himself at a Burns Supper as "the Messiah" then added: "I must be, as only this morning a miscreant led into the dock looked up at the bench and muttered, 'It's him! Jesus Christ!'"

THE Diary story about the US consulate in Edinburgh reminds Bruce Skivington: "The consulate is at 3 Regent Terrace, just along from the old Royal High School. In the 1960s the house at Number 4 was used by the RHS as a classroom. When the US nuclear Polaris submarines arrived at the Holy Loch, anti-nuclear protesters laid down on the pavement outside the consulate, and the police arrived with a wily sergeant telling consulate staff to wait and see.

"At 11am the school bell rang for morning break, and out poured a tsunami of black blazers heading at high speed to be first in the milk queue in the old school playground. House 4 had over 100 thirsty pupils who had to pass the consulate and would stop at nothing. When the dust settled the trampled protesters decided to continue the protest across the road."

SOMETIMES people want to avoid doing their civic duty. As one reader tells us: "If you get called for jury duty and want to get out of it, just wait until the charges are read out at the beginning of the trial, then yell out: 'Oh come on. Even I've done that.'"

SEEMINGLY it was National Badger Day yesterday, which reminds us of the English police force which was trying to cut crime figures by talking folk out of reporting crimes. An officer went to a house where the occupants claimed they had been broken into and showed the officer scratch marks on their patio doors. "Could have been a badger," he told them. However they pointed out that their 42-inch TV was missing.

"Must have been two of them," replied the officer.

OUR story of protesters at the US Consulate reminds Lachlan Bradley: "I helped organise a teachers' rally in Ayr in the 1980s where, at the Low Green, a minibus arrived and a number of young police officers disembarked. One of them said to the sergeant, 'Are we expecting any trouble today Sarge?' The sergeant gave him a withering look and replied, 'Son, they are teachers. If you blow a whistle they'll all line up in twos'."

WE mentioned the death of Glasgow Sheriff J Irvine Smith, and a lawyer passes on: "He was trying a drink-driving case where the accused has been aggressive and offensive with the traffic polis.

"Found guilty, the accused launches into a long monologue, begging not to be disqualified.

"When he finishes, Irvine looks gravely at him over his half-moons and says, 'Go and take a f*** to yersel' and 'This a just a load of s****!' Stunned silence in courtroom, many thinking the learned sheriff has finally lost it, only for him to continue, 'That's what you said to the officers when they

asked you to give a breath test. I can find no room for special reasons'."

THE second day of the legal submissions in MP Alistair Carmichael's court case ploughed on, filmed live on television, without, it has to be said, the excitement of a *Law & Order* episode. Even Mr Carmichael wisely didn't turn up. As one observer eventually remarked on social media: "This is borin'. Ah want Carmichael on the stand shoutin', 'Youse waant the truth? Youse cannie haunel the truth!'"

IT wasn't all bad though as the Diary's favourite judge, Kilmarnock lad Lord Matthews, still has his sense of humour. As Mr Carmichael's QC claimed that if the petitioners prevailed, politicians would have to be strapped to a lie detector and administered a truth serum, Lord M asked with a smile on his face: "Is that a bad thing?"

BLACK pudding, apparently packed with protein, calcium, potassium and iron, is said to be the new superfood. Who knew? We recall the reader who told us about a vital Dundee v Celtic game when the fans were jostling outside the ground and someone threw a black pudding supper which hit a big policeman on the face.

Despite being in the mould of PC Murdoch from *Oor Wullie*, he moved at breakneck speed, rounded up those in the vicinity, and, although all denied involvement, he demanded everyone "show us yer teeth". The chap with the offending remains of black pudding on his molars was spotted, and quickly huckled into the nearest police van.

SHERIFF Smith's love of poetry even extended to his sentencing. A recidivist named Barney Noone always addressed the bench in verse, so Irvine followed suit by sentencing him thus: "Thirty days hath November, April, June and Barney Noone."

"HOW is it," asked a chap in a Glasgow pub the other night: "that a theme park can snap a clear pic of you at 70 mph, but a bank's security camera can't get a clear picture of a robber standing still?"

GOOD to see these local community Facebook pages where folk can help each other. The one for Clarkston on Glasgow's South Side includes the plea: "We have a garden shed that needs to be cleared out and the contents disposed of and then dismantled. Wondered if anyone knows who could help with this please?" A weary local replied: "Don't know. But if you leave it unlocked I'm sure someone will pinch whatever is inside. Happened to half the houses in our street, and even when they were padlocked."

WE had brought the curtain down on our Sheriff Irvine Smith stories, but we are happy to leave the last word to entertainer Andy Cameron who reminds us: "My favourite of his was where there was a person in the public gallery chewing gum so loudly that it could be heard two courts away.

"The Sheriff told the Clerk of the Court to tell the person to 'stop masticating' whereupon the wee Clerk approached the public gallery and instructed the offender, 'the Sherriff says ye've to take your hauns oot yer pockets'."

6
Politics

Where to start? It's been such a turbulent year in politics that having a laugh seems the only way of coping with it.

INTERESTING developments in Scottish politics at the weekend. As Ramsay Urquhart of UKIP put it: "Kezia Dugdale has been elected the new Scottish Labour leader. For those of you asking, 'Who?', it's a political party."

MUCH-lambasted Tony Abbott has lost the leadership of his party and will be replaced as Australia's PM. In one of his many gaffes he once described the opposition as being "a bit like the Irishman who lost 10 pounds betting on the Grand National and then lost 20 pounds on the action replay". The Irish Embassy asked him to apologise.

STILL lots of attacks in the media on Jeremy Corbyn and the

prospect of him becoming Labour leader. A confused Stephen Law tells us: "It seems that over 20 years, without changing my political views much, if at all, I've moved from mainstream Labour to Loony Left."

WE bump into an old trade unionist chum in Buchanan Street who unzips his jacket, despite the freezing weather, to show us his new T-shirt. It is red and has the word "Labour" emblazoned on it. Below in smaller letters it adds: "Prefer their early work".

WE read in *The Herald* that Tommy Sheridan has launched his bid to be elected again to the Scottish Parliament. We suspect some of the MSPs have missed him, as we recall Labour's Neil Findlay once interrupting a speech by the SNP's Mike Russell and Mike retorting: "When Neil Findlay intervened, we were hearing an echo of Tommy Sheridan talking about class war. I knew, and was not a great supporter of, Tommy Sheridan. Mr Findlay is no Tommy Sheridan."

Neil at least had the comeback: "The wife will be pleased!"

STV'S Holyrood editor Colin Mackay, who MC'd *The Herald's* Politician Of The Year awards, revealed to the audience in his review of the year: "When Nicola Sturgeon met the Queen as First Minster at Buckingham Palace there was some discussion over whether she should curtsy or not. Nicola said just please yourself."

And on the question of another referendum on independence,

Colin explained: "In her conference speech Nicola said we will have to wait until something significant has changed before another referendum. Given the age of No voters, she might mean a couple of really bad winters."

RESIGNING UK Government minister Iain Duncan Smith is much in the news. My colleague David Leask recalls: "The only time I saw IDS in Glasgow, a lass with a bald wean yelled, 'Oi Tory boy! See the last time you were here!' and pointed in her pram."

AND our tale about George Foulkes standing in a previous election with the poster "For Foulkes' sake - Vote Labour" reminds David Will in Milngavie: "I penned a slogan in the Eighties for a Tory candidate standing for the Glasgow seat in the European Parliament which was held by the late Janey Buchan from 1979 to 1994. The slogan, 'Never forget, there is a Buchan alternative', was never adopted."

TALKING of Westminster, fellow SNP MP John Nicholson has tongue in cheek as he brings the latest shocking news to social media and states: "Good God. There's a chap at the despatch box in the Commons wearing corduroys. The barbarians are at the door."

AND journalist Alan Woodison reflects: "The utterances of the late and lamented Irvine councillor Jack Carson were indecipherable, gravel-voiced retorts which were legendary at council meetings.

"The *Irvine Times*, after their customary Monday morning phone chat with 'Wee Jack', stated in a headline that he was at a waste management conference in Turkey. Then explained the following week, in a tiny, bottom-of-the-page paragraph, that he had actually been in Torquay."

THE news that many of Scotland's political leaders are homosexual has piqued interest in the world's media, and Scottish-based crime writer Val McDermid was asked by the *Guardian* newspaper to write an article about it, in which she stated: "John Knox must be birling in his box like a peerie."

The sentence was asterisked by the newspaper and at the bottom of the article it explained: "John Knox (founder of Scottish Protestantism) must be spinning in his grave like a top."

WE mentioned the late man-of-the-people Renfrewshire Labour MP Tommy Graham and we are reminded of the time he was with a crowd of MPs in the House of Commons Travel Office trying to discover if planes to Glasgow were flying because of the bad weather. As his former colleague Brian Donohoe recalled: "Tommy called his long-suffering wife Joan and asked her to go upstairs - they stayed in Linwood - to look out the window and see if the planes were landing.

"After a wee while she came back to say, 'Aye Tommy, they're landing', so we all rushed to book the last plane to Glasgow.

"At the counter was an Edinburgh Tory who inquired if Tommy knew if the planes were landing at Edinburgh. 'Haud on son,' replied Tommy in his inimitable style. 'I'll get the wife to climb on tap o' the wardrobe an see if they're landing at Edinburgh'."

IT can be amusing when politicians take to social media. Glasgow Southside SNP MP Stewart McDonald thundered yesterday: "This Friday is International Hummus Day in London. The fact that this is a thing brings shame on our country." Glasgow writer Edwin Moore gently replied: "Stewart, it's hummus, not Hamas."

CONGRATULATIONS to Ken Macintosh becoming the new presiding officer at the Scottish Parliament. Ken showed his unflappable side when he was one of three candidates to lead the Scottish Labour party a few years back, and Labour leader Ed Miliband, embarrassingly, couldn't remember his name. When asked about it by a journalist, father-of-six Ken replied: "I don't think anyone should read anything into it - half the time I can't remember the names of my own kids."

OH and Labour leader Kezia Dugdale can come across as a bit whiny at times, so we commend her touch of humour when she remarked about the new SNP Government: "I congratulate the First Minister on once again securing a gender-balanced Cabinet. I warn her though that if she continues to insist on a 50/50 split in her Cabinets, she will have to convince Parliament that the men are all there on their merits."

TWO SNP MPs, Stewart Hosie and Angus MacNeil, are in the news for both having affairs with Westminster journalist Serena Cowdy. As many people wonder what she saw in them, we turn to Serena's blog where she recently wrote: "I am a bona fide nut magnet. If there's someone who is in any way eccentric, unstable, drunk, on drugs, or otherwise misfiring socially, you can absolutely guarantee they will gravitate towards me."

Glad to have cleared that up.

BRIAN Whittle, athlete turned politician, who won the gold medal in the relay at both the 1986 and 1994 European Championships, has taken his seat at the Scottish Parliament as a Tory MSP. As he told the other MSPs in his maiden speech this week: "I was an international athlete for 13 years. To those members who have mentioned it, I say thank you for remembering. Those who said, 'I do not remember you, but my dad said that you were not bad,' have made a happy man feel old."

SCOTTISH Tory leader Ruth Davidson asked her followers on social media yesterday: "Anyone else think that the Sky sub-editors have started 'Bring a Euphemism to Work Day'? The reason for her question was the headline on Sky News "Woman accused of sabotaging her fiance's kayak says she removed its plug and manipulated his paddle."

JOHN Park in Lanarkshire swears to us: "I was in a shop behind a Polish couple, and the till girl asked if they wanted help packing their bags. The fella says, 'Not yet. The EU vote was only on Thursday'."

BEN Wright's just published book *Order! Order! The Rise and Fall of Political Drinking* explores how alcohol has affected politicians, and as you might imagine, includes the classic tale of Labour's Foreign Secretary George Brown on a trip to Brazil making a beeline for a gorgeously crimson-clad figure at a drinks reception for visiting dignitaries from Peru, and asking for a dance. He was told: "There are three reasons why I will not dance with you. First, I fear you are drunk. Secondly, that is not a waltz the orchestra is playing but Peru's national anthem. And thirdly, I am the Archbishop of Lima."

Author Ben Wright observes: "The one small caveat to this magnificent tale is that it is probably not true."

SOME folk feel the politics of the last few days following the European referendum feels more like a bizarre joke, so perhaps it was inevitable someone turned it into a classic one by stating: "An Englishman, an Irishman and a Scotsman, walked into a bar. But they all had to leave when the Englishman said he wanted to go."

WE try to make sense of the American presidential elections. An American tells us: "I heard someone say that they like Donald Trump 'because he isn't a politician'. So I had to tell him that makes as much sense as saying you prefer to call an electrician when your toilet breaks down."

AND a reader down south emails to explain: "I was hosting a barbecue at the weekend for some old racist Leave voters. I wouldn't normally on principle, but one of them gave birth to me and the other watched."

THE *New York Times* reported that Presidential candidate Donald Trump is demanding $10,000 for any journalist to accompany him to Scotland this week for the reopening of the Ailsa golf course at Trump's Turnberry Hotel.

We know there is a debate about whether Americans get irony, but at least one of them gets sarcasm, as a Californian reader told the *Times*: "Please *New York Times* cover this important event. As far as the cost, readers will be more than happy to pay a bit more for our subscriptions to read about it."

FINALLY, we go back on our word about no more light bulb jokes, with James Bethell asking us: "How many Brexiters does it take to change a light bulb?" "Hold on a minute, we never said there'd be a light bulb."

BUT perhaps we are over-thinking this. We turn to social media for a bit of clarity where Connor Magill in Ayr states: "Wit if Scotland just refuses to leave the EU? Like, aw just say naw, 'n' tell England, 'Wit ye gonny dae? Phone the polis?'"

IT was the Royal Highland Show at Ingliston, and David McVey in Milton of Campsie tells us: "Two chaps wearing sombreros went past, I think they were from a promotional stand. A couple were going the other way and the wife said to the husband, 'Is that some anti-Trump statement?'" And we liked the folk singer appearing on stage at the show who stopped between songs to retune his banjo, and announced: "Sorry about this. It's a Scottish instrument, it's not used to the sunshine."

INTERESTING times. A South Side reader on holiday in Berlin at the weekend was stopped by a German TV crew seeking out Brits to ask them about the vote to leave the EU.

He tells us: "I told the wee man that I didn't speak German. In fact the only German I know is what I learned from *Commando* comics in my youth, which is 'Verdant Englanders!' and 'Gott im Himmel!'. Now I think about it, these two phrases would pretty much have covered it in the interview."

SO Boris is not standing. It was summed up by one reader who tells us: "Feels a bit like Boris took the UK for a test drive, crashed it into a wall, and then brought it back to the garage saying, 'I don't want it. It's dented'."

7

The View from Abroad

In case we get too insular, we always like to see how folk abroad view Scotland, and how Scots cope when they get on a plane to sample other cultures.

A READER in Winnipeg, Canada, passes on a story from local newspaper columnist Doug Speirs who was compering a children's charity picnic when he was joined on stage by some Scottish dancers and their piper.

Doug told the audience his only piper joke which was: "I heard on the news that terrorists have captured a plane loaded with bagpipers. And if their demands aren't met, they're going to let one piper go every hour."

Doug just found it odd that someone complained to his editor that he was telling children jokes about terrorists, rather than anyone complaining about jokes about bagpipes.

THE controversial taxi service Uber, which calls a minicab, but only from a smart phone, has come to Glasgow. We remember an American sailor discussing Uber in the States and passing on: "My buddy Dean grabbed an Uber from a Muslim driver. When he got in, the driver asked if he was Christian. Dean from South Carolina said, 'Hell, yeah I'm a Christian!'. About a mile down the road the driver gets a call from a guy called Christian wondering who got into his Uber."

SO how chatty do you like your shop assistants to be? A reader visiting relatives in Surrey was in a local shop where the young chap behind the counter said with an American accent to a stiff-backed local: "Hi there. How are you doing today?" The elderly chap merely replied: "You're not in America now, so you can keep that to yourself."

A READER sends us a cutting from the *Lewisboro Ledger* newspaper in New York State which has a "Police Blotter" column in which more minor events involving the police are recorded.

The story states: "Trespassing reported on Grandview Terrace, South Salem. Caller reported that she thought her drunk neighbour was playing music in her garage. The officer found that it was the caller's husband in the garage and that the caller did not know her husband was home at the time."

Come on, it could happen to anyone.

AS others see us. A reader in America sends us a cutting from his local newspaper's funny page which includes: "A waiter held a tray at a Scottish party and the guest looked at the little sticks with ham and cheese and asked, 'Canapé?' The Scottish waiter replied, 'No, you're all right. They're free'."

A READER in America tells us her local newspaper was running a piece on unwelcome house guests. A reader responded with the succinct story: "Buddy used to pee out a second-storey window to avoid going to the downstairs bathroom. One time he did and the sunroof on my mother's Lexus was open below."

AS readers return from holidays abroad, Ron Evans tried not to rub it in by telling us he was in Louisiana where the heat was so intense that he asked an officer in a police patrol car if it was OK to pull over onto the hard shoulder for a quick nap. The officer came back with the memorable response: "Sure thing man, I would rather wake you up than scrape you up!"

TALKING of America, it is now more than 25 years since deadbeat dad Homer Simpson first appeared on television.

As one American commented: "Sad that 25 years ago Homer Simpson seemed like a loser in American culture, but nowadays folk are impressed that he not only has a job but owns his home."

OUR mention of the submarines being built on the Clyde in the 1970s for Chile reminds Callum Satchel in Dunoon: "I met a Chilean ex-naval officer in Chile, and he said he knew Greenock, as he had been standing by the submarines being built there. When I asked what he thought of the town he replied, 'I slept in one Saturday, missed the summer!'"

AS others see us. We mentioned a joke about Scots printed in an American newspaper. A reader sends us another American newspaper clipping which states: "Do you know the first people in the UK to have double glazing were the Scots? It was so their bairns couldn't hear the ice cream vans."

ALSO in America, a reader sends us a copy of a survey where tourists to the USA are asked what strikes them as strange about the country. One chap replied: "I guess one thing that's odd is that the average American seems a lot more attuned to the outdoors than we are. I've seen Americans sporadically ask their friends if they want to go on a night hike or go hunting. Generally if you hunt animals in the UK you're part of the nobility."

AH the dangers of social media. An American reader tells us a local store got a call from a customer saying the guitar he had ordered did not arrive, and he wanted a replacement or his money back. On a whim a member of staff looked up the customer on Facebook where he had posted a picture of himself holding a guitar with the caption: "My new guitar just arrived."

Management simply emailed him the picture and never heard from him again.

TODAY'S piece of whimsy comes from Joe Knox who declared: "I was told if it's raining in Denmark you have to drive with headlights switched on. The question is, how do I find out if it's raining in Denmark?"

8

Technology

New technology, social media - all have had a profound affect on our lives. Fortunately some of our readers could also see the funny side of it.

WISE words from a colleague who tells us: "Just watched a five-minute video of a dog going round and round in circles chasing its own tail, and I chuckled to myself about how easily amused it was. And then I realised I had watched the whole five-minute video."

A READER phones to tell us: "Accidentally put my phone on airplane mode and within minutes a fat businessman wedged himself next to me on the sofa, and a child started kicking the back of my seat."

WE forget sometimes how quickly things change. Still Game

actor Sanjeev Kohli pointed out yesterday: "Watching an episode of *Friends* with the kids, and Ross has a pager. It inspired the same reaction as a Victorian mangle on a school trip."

INTERESTING what social media throws up. A young chap in Fife has explained: "My maw has just put two quid under ma wee brother's pillow cause his tooth fell out, and av stole it cause av nae money to get to college the morra."

SOME of our readers are a bit fed up with the intrusiveness of technology in their lives these days. However, one Glasgow reader summed it up by emailing us: "What did our parents do when they were bored before the internet was invented, I asked my 11 siblings. They didn't know either."

TALKING of social media, Craig Deeley sums it up for some people with the conversation: "Did you get my text?" "Yes, but I've been in a massive car accident. I'm in the ambulance now." "Phew! I thought you were ignoring me."

ASKED where the colleague who usually ambushes me with jokes was yesterday. Was told he had taken some time off to go shopping with his wife. He eventually texted me to say: "Currently in the 'men staring intently at mobile phones' section of Dorothy Perkins."

EVER sold anything second-hand over the Internet? A reader sends us a comment from one such site in Brighton where a local posts a picture of a young man, and comments: "Warning. This guy was supposed to buy our washer-dryer machine for £150. He wanted to see it working first and asked if he could do a load of laundry. After he finished he said, 'Let me go and get the money'. Got in his car and drove away with his clean clothes."

TALKING of social media, we pass on the message posted by American TV station NBC News which stated: "Isis fighters are shaving bears and hiding in civilian homes to avoid air strikes."

Two minutes later it added: "Correction: it was beards, not bears."

A GLASGOW reader tells us she received a surprise text message from her boyfriend who was at work, which stated: "Please ignore this text, I'm just pretending to add a person's phone number to my address book."

GLASGOW'S marketing folk use the phrase "People Make Glasgow" in order to promote the city. And a great job they do too. Just occasionally though folk use the phrase "People Make Glasgow" on the social media site Twitter to paint a slightly different picture. All done with warmth though, we are sure. Among the latest comments are:

   *Just witnessed a guy trying to pick a fight with a moving bus (Ross Jardine).

   *Can't believe some guy came up to me in Queen Street and zipped my jacket up. Never said a word, just zipped it up (Dominic Donaldson).

   *Genuinely just seen someone drinking from a puddle like a dog (Joanne Molloy).

"WHY do you not do a low calorie Tennent's lager? Or a Tennent's lite?" a customer asked Glasgow brewery Tennent's on Twitter.

   Never stuck for words, Tennent's Lager posted the reply: "We do, mate - it's called a half pint."

HARD being a teenager these days it seems. A Whitecraigs reader was on the train into Glasgow when he heard a teenage girl in the carriage heavily sigh and tell her pal: "I'm like an iPhone. I don't do anything and still all my energy drains away."

TALKING of social media, Alec Ross in Lochans passes on: "A friend muses, 'Remember when we used to make pumpkin lanterns, take pictures of them, and then take the photos round all our friends' houses?' Nope, me neither".

A HYNDLAND reader is still puzzling over a text he received from his wife, which stated: "It's sad that everyone on the Subway is just sitting here staring at their phones." He wonders how she could have sent it without sitting there staring at her phone.

SOME men just don't react the right way when colleagues start discussing welcome additions to their family. Says Simon Caine: "Someone just showed me a photo of their baby on their mobile, and my first response was, 'Why are you still using an iPhone 4?'"

WE mentioned the teacher who, when asking about a pupil's homework, was told it was "still in the pen". Reader Bruce Skivington asks: "Surely these days the answer to, 'Where is your homework?' is, 'It's still on Google'."

A READER swears to us he heard a chap in a Glasgow boozer at the weekend tell his pals: "My credit card company sent me a final notice. Good, I was tired of hearing from them."

A SOUTH Side reader swears to us that a young girl got on his train to Glasgow the other day, slumped on to a seat, and told her pals: "I only left the house today so that my selfies would have different backgrounds."

THERE are downsides to so many folk carrying camera phones these days. A reader emails to ask: "What's the new etiquette rule? Am I supposed to wait until everyone is done photographing their meals before I start eating mine?"

OCCASIONAL stories on dealing with phone calls from your mother, continued. Says Simon Caine: "Today I learned making up fake emergencies to get your mum off the phone only leads to more phone calls."

9

Older But Not Always Wiser

One of the delights of growing older is the realisation that it does not actually make you any wiser, and that you are just as daft as you ever were.

A SLICE of life we must pass on from reader Barrie Crawford who says: "Just back from my daily swim at the local baths. There is a group of three or four retired men who are there just about every day. They swim slowly up and down discussing last night's TV, the news and generally putting the world to rights. I think of them as a floating *Still Game*. Today, however, there was only one of them. He swam towards me and said, 'All my pals have deserted me this morning. I'm floating about here like a wee lost jobby'."

A CUMBERNAULD reader is already worrying about turning 40 in a couple of years. Her mood wasn't helped when she went for a drink after work with colleagues to a place where a doorman was checking ages. A 23-year-old colleague asked our reader to her great dismay: "I've no ID with me. Will you pretend to be my mum and tell them I'm old enough?"

A READER swears to us he was visiting a relative in a care home where patients are given a wrist band detailing anything they are allergic to so that any new staff knows what they can take. He says there was a bit of a row when a son living abroad came to visit his mother, did not know the system, and buttonholed a member of staff to angrily ask: "Which one of you labelled my mother 'bananas'?"

COLD-CALLING continued. Says Cora Adcock: "A local firm of solicitors rang me to ask whether I had made a will. I got rid of them by replying, 'Aye, I have - but I'm afraid you're no' in it'."

OUR story about ancient underwear reminds us that Scottish author Margaret Thomson Davis once told a writers' group that she often scribbled down snatches of conversation overheard on buses, including one between two women in the 1960s who had recently bought themselves nylon nighties, after years of wearing flannelette ones. 'What do you think of your new nylon nightie, Jenny?' 'I don't like it, May - I can see my semmit through it'.

WISE words from a Pollokshields reader about growing old. She tells us: "One way to find out if you're old is to fall down in front of a group of people. If they laugh, you're young. If they panic, you're old."

AN AYRSHIRE reader tells us he noticed in his quiet cul-de-sac that the daughter of the elderly woman who lived opposite was visiting the house every evening when she normally only appeared once at the weekend. He went on: "Fearing for the health of the elderly lady, my wife phoned across, steeling her-self for bad news. The elderly woman picks it up, and when my wife voices concern for her health, the old lady explains, 'My daughter's washing machine has broken down. She's round every night to use ours'."

CHRISTMAS present buying, and a reader remembers last year when she tried to persuade her aged mum on the benefits of computers. When her mum asked what would she do with one, our reader told her that she could go on Facebook, and keep in touch with her friends.

"At my age," replied her mum, "I'd need a ouija board."

WE often contemplate the changes in our lives when we get older. As Glasgow stand-up Susan Calman put it: "Cheered and clapped when my boiler passed a safety inspection. The 16-year-old me would be astounded at what makes the 40-year-old me happy."

LYNN McConnell was in a shop in Biggar, Lanarkshire, where a young woman and her elderly mother were perusing a painting for sale. The dubious daughter remarked: "I'm not too sure about it. Maybe Dad would like it?" Her mum replied: "Well it's no' my piece of cake."

"Do you mean cup of tea Mum?" asked the daughter. "No, I think I will just wait until we are home," said mum.

Says Lynn: "The daughter just walked away laughing."

GROWING old continued. Says Moose Allain: "The good thing when you get to my age is that you don't get hangovers any more - because you feel like this all the time."

MORE signs you are getting old. A reader back from holiday in America tells us: "I was horrified to discover I was humming along to the music being played in my hotel lift. It's all downhill from now."

10

What are we working for?

We spend so much of our lives at work that it is bound to throw up a story or two. Here are a few of them.

A READER says he is not sure if this is the circle of life people go on about, but he heard a fellow customer in a Clydebank bar the other week bemoan: "I hate my job, but it pays for my drink. And I need to drink because I hate my job."

A COLLEAGUE feels the need to catch our attention and tells us: "Before I got into journalism I was made redundant from a helium manufacturing factory. They still speak highly of me."

A GLASGOW reader tells us that his firm had sent him along to one of those business meetings with an inspirational speaker. The chap was working up a head of steam when he asked the audience: "What do we do in Scotland better than anyone else?" His talk was spoiled somewhat by someone shouting out: "Rain".

A READER reminiscing about the changes in his job over the years tells us: "If I could tell my 12-year-old self that my job in the future would involved using passwords every day, I fear he would think it was going to be a lot more exciting than it actually is."

OUR mention of ice-cream vans being overly optimistic in the current Scottish weather takes Malcolm Boyd in Milngavie far, far down memory lane. He tells us: "My late father-in-law, who was of Italian extraction, operated an ice-cream van after the war, and during one bad winter he drove to Kilbowie Roundabout, Clydebank, and rang his bell.

"The snow was falling heavily as a door opened, and a man wrapped in a heavy overcoat came out and trudged through the snow to the van. He asked, 'Are you selling ice cream?' My father-in-law answered yes in anticipation of a large order but the man just told him, 'You're bloody mad!' before trudging back into his house."

WE'VE not had nicknames for a while, and Robert Mackie tells us: "In Yarrow's we had one engineer foreman who was called Danny Kaye because his response to being asked anything mildly out of the ordinary was, 'Ah canny dae that'."

QUESTIONS for speakers, continued. Head of employee relations at Scottish Engineering, Raymond Lowe, was running an employment law course in England when he was asked about employees stealing. Says Raymond: "I told them about when I took a 2lb bag of sugar into work on a Monday morning and found it was gone on Tuesday. We thought the nightshift was making tablet!

"I asked at the end of the two-day course if there were any questions to which I was asked, 'What is tablet?'"

THE charity RSABI, which helps relieve hardship amongst farm workers, is selling the light-hearted book *Farming Is A Funny Business* by Andrew and John Arbuckle to raise funds. In it we hear of the farmer's wife who told a friend she was going to Venice. "Oh, lovely," her friend said, "is it a romantic trip?" "No," the farmer's wife told her, "I'm going with my husband."

WE mentioned interactions with bosses, and Malcolm Boys in Milngavie recalls: "When I worked at the British Leyland

Albion Plant in Scotstoun, a story circulated about the chairman, on a visit, stopping to speak to a junior member of staff. 'Do you have far to travel to work?' he asked. 'No, I live on an estate in the north of Glasgow' replied the lad. 'Do you keep horses?' asked the chairman."

THE office Christmas parties continue, and a reader hears a drunken blow-hard in a Glasgow pub trying to impress a young woman with: "I made six figures last year."

But she merely replied: "What? Are you a really slow worker in a toy factory?"

OUR story about haughty bosses reminds David Noble in Ayr of when he were a lad and had to pick up his boss who was dropping his Range Rover off at the garage for a service. His boss climbed into David's 12-year-old Opel and remarked: "You like these old classic cars, don't you?" Says David: "I didn't have the heart to tell him that on my meagre wages, it was all I could afford."

WORKPLACE nicknames continued. "I used to have a steel erector who was nicknamed 'Blister'," says Ian Petrie. "He only appeared after the hard work was done."

YES, office party time, and a reader in Glasgow heard a chap in the bar tell a female colleague who had got glammed up for the occasion: "You look better when you don't wear your glasses."

She gave him a bit of a stare before replying: "Funnily enough you look better when I don't wear my glasses as well."

ICE cream vans. Is it just me, or are there fewer of them on the roads these days? Anyway Andy Cumming tells us: "Talking to a work colleague who told me he bought an old ice-cream van to use to deliver his fresh fish door to door in Lanarkshire in the 1980s. He said he left the original chimes intact to sound his arrival. Used to drive the kids nuts."

WORK nicknames continued: "We had a colleague known to us all as 'Crime' as he used to follow the police guidance that 'Crime does not pay' on every visit to the pub," says Harry Clark in Bishopbriggs.

AH, the working man as art critic. Architectural historian Barnabas Calder writes of his love of brutalist architecture in his just published book *Raw Concrete*. He tells of the partial demolition of Paisley Civic Centre in 2010, and how he managed to save a section from the rubble. When he was then moving out of Glasgow he told movers it was a fragile ornament. It was well packaged, he concedes, but the removal man wrote "lump o' concrete" on the label. Says Barnabas: "When I explained what it was, he crossed out his label and wrote instead, 'Precious relic of car park'."

A TALE of two cities. Sausage-roll sellers Greggs is closing its Edinburgh bakery, but expanding its Glasgow one. It reminds us of the chap in Glasgow who was asked by a visiting journalist before the independence referendum if he was concerned about businesses pulling out of Scotland if there was a Yes vote. "Only if it was Greggs," he replied.

And the gag: "My wife put her hair in a bun this morning," said the chap in Glasgow. "That's why she got sacked from Greggs."

OH dear, a colleague wanders over, wanting to talk about his jobs before he went into journalism.

"I secretly resigned from my job as a set designer," he said. "I didn't want to make a scene."

WORKPLACE nicknames continued. Says Stuart Roberts in Switzerland: "At Rolls-Royce in East Kilbride one of the folks in the office, from Paisley, earned the name 'diesel' as every time the stationery cupboard was unlocked he would appear and take pens and pencils while intimating, 'diesel dae fur the kids'."

A DIARY story last week commented on a Glasgow company making bulletproof sofas, and a reader swears to us his mum read the story and asked: "Why would a sofa have so many enemies?"

THE Herald's archive picture of the old Meadowside Granary reminds Hugh Steele in Cumbernauld: "I worked in the offices there for about 14 years, and we found a forgotten store room which had a box of old chunky brass lapel badges advertising that you worked for the Clyde Navigation Trust. The badge simply said 'CNT'. As you can imagine, no-one was keen on wearing such a logo into a Partick pub."

IT reminds us of a former colleague who recently moved house who had many a cardboard box full of books, which the removal men struggled with down the stairs of one flat and up the stairs of where he had moved. Eventually after taking the umpteenth box up the stairs, the removal man remarked: "Have you ever thought of getting a Kindle?"

WE asked for your removal stories and James Laughlan passes on: "Local removal man in Larkhall was asked to do a flitting for an old man, with all his goods to be transported to another house nearby, including his Doocot. The shed was easily dismantled and moved. The 'doos' were more difficult, with the removal man trying to catch dozens of them fluttering all over the street, rather than letting them work it out for themselves."

DRESS codes are changing it seems. A Glasgow reader had to smile when his boss, always at his desk in suit, shirt and tie, had to go through to Edinburgh for a meeting with a computer systems company. He came back, shook his head, and gave the memorable comment: "They obviously have a different office dress code - most of the people looked like they were off to a barbecue, or maybe on their way to clear out a lock-up."

BP shareholders voted against a massive pay rise for chief executive Bob Dudley that would take his annual salary to more than £13m. A reader phones to explain: "Dudley has hit back saying he needs the money to be able to afford some crisps and a drink for the family when he pays for his petrol in a BP station."

OTHER school-leavers are of course entering the jobs market just now. A reader who works in HR says he wonders how accurate a job-seeker was being when he wrote on an application form: "I am reaching my goals, slowly but surly."

A DIARY story about mistaking someone's intentions reminds reader Ron Hanvey: "When I was a young probation officer in Glasgow, I was summoned after only six months to see the chief probation officer in his office on the top floor. I assumed my greatness had prematurely been recognised and I was on the fast track for promotion.

"On being greeted amicably by the great man himself I sat back and waited with bated breath on the good news. Unknown to me he had scanned the application forms of all probation officers to find out their previous employment. This soon became apparent, as he asked me how soon I could come to his home to repair his leaking toilet bowl."

NOW that the grass-cutting season is well under way, we learn from a Kintyre reader of a vertically-challenged streetwise chap named Morrison who supplements his dole money by keeping various gardens ship-shape. He had acquired the nickname of Wee Fly Mo.

A COMPANY boss in Glasgow tells us he was interviewing a chap for a job the other week and asked him the standard question: "Tell me a little about yourself." However, the interviewee shifted in his chair and replied: "I'd rather not - I'm quite keen to get this job."

OUR tale of the chap digging gardens while collecting unemployment reminds John Crawford in Lytham: "East Ayrshire Council required all window cleaners to have a Civic Government Licence. We had an anonymous report about a bloke who was cleaning windows without having a licence. An investigation revealed he was in his late 70s and cleaned the windows of all his elderly widowed neighbours in return for a plate of soup on weekdays.

"So we let him carry on."

WE MENTIONED how a child in the sixties would think a job in the future that used passwords every day would be more exciting than it actually is, prompting a reader to muse: "If someone from the sixties appeared today, do you know what the most difficult thing to explain would be? Possessing a device that fits in your pocket on which you can access all the information ever known to man. But you use it to look at pictures of cats and to get into arguments with strangers."

A HAMILTON reader was in a local shop where a regular was telling the staff that he had taken early retirement.

The woman chatting with him asked: "So is there nothing you miss about not going into work?" After thinking about it for a few seconds all he could come up with was: "Sometimes when it was someone's birthday you got a bit of free cake."

A READER on the train into Glasgow heard a fellow Southsider ask her pal: "Have you ever been told something, but you can't decide if it's a compliment or an insult?" When her pal asked what she meant, the woman added: "When I went into work yesterday in a new summer dress, a colleague said to me, 'You look so gorgeous, I didn't recognise you!'"

11
Relationships

The course of true love does not always run smoothly - and when it doesn't who better to tell than *The Herald Diary?*

A GLASGOW woman is heard telling her pals: "My husband took me out for dinner on our anniversary. I tried to get him to be all romantic during the meal and I asked him to tell me something that would make my heart beat faster.

"So he told me he'd forgotten to bring his credit card."

A READER swears to us he was out in Glasgow's west end with a mate who went to chat to a young woman further along the bar. After a while he came back and told him: "She studies psychology at the uni. She claims I'm a narcissist who misjudges social situations. Do you think she's trying to get off with me?"

WISE words in a Glasgow pub overheard the other night where an older chap was giving relationship advice to some young drinkers. "If a woman asks if she looks fat," he told them, "it's not enough to say 'No'. You must also act very surprised by the question. Jump backwards if necessary."

A READER hears a woman in a Glasgow coffee shop tell her pals: "My husband said he would unload the dishwasher. 'No rush,' I told him. That was three days ago and it's still full."

ACTUALLY, a reader overheard Valentine's Day being discussed in a Glasgow pub where one single lad eventually asked a married chap sitting near the bar what it was like being hitched.

The older chap thought for a moment before replying: "Marriage is mostly about knowing which hand towels you can use, and which ones are to be left for people better than you when they visit the house."

IT appears that some folk on dating sites tend to gild the lily a little by using older pictures of themselves. One chap was heard in a Glasgow pub telling his pals after some disastrous dates: "Do you think it's rude if I ask the next woman I see on a dating site if she could send a picture of herself holding up a copy of today's paper?"

HAVING a pint in a Glasgow pub at the weekend, a reader hears a young chap argue with his pals: "I don't get my girlfriend. One minute she says I'm a typical man and can't multi-task, the next she's accusing me of seeing another woman behind her back. Which is it?"

A SOUTH Side reader confesses that he made a face when his wife told him they were going to a family gathering this Easter, and she declared: "You don't like any of my relatives, do you?" He felt that his answer of: "That's not true. I like your mother-in-law far more than mine" was inspired, even though it got him into even more trouble.

A READER in a Glasgow pub at the weekend heard a young chap explain to his pals: "I met a girl at a club last night who told me she'd show me a good time." After a suitable pause to get attention, he then added: "When we got outside she ran a hundred yards in under 12 seconds."

THESE online reviews of products can throw up the occasional gem. Mike Ritchie on Glasgow's South Side tells us: "My wife is thinking of buying a cooker range so was checking online reviews of various models. One chap - Douglas from Johnstone to be exact - had a pithy view on the matter of the new cooker installed. 'Works well, looks good, just need the wife to turn it on more often'."

NO SOONER are we back from our holidays when a colleague spots us and lumbers over to engage us with: "My girlfriend wrote on a balloon 'Will you propose to me?'. I immediately popped the question."

A READER swears to us that he heard a woman in a Glasgow bar tell her pals when they were discussing their respective partners: "My husband's my rock.
   "He just sits around the house doing nothing."

SO we bump into a misogynist in a Glasgow pub the other night who declares: "We had friends round for dinner the other night, and the wife called me into the kitchen and told me to prepare the table.

"So I went into the dining room and explained to our guests about her cooking."

A COLLEAGUE wanders over to give us advice, and states: "Always be yourself. Unless you run into one of your exes. Then you have to be a way more successful version of yourself."

A READER asked a pal in a Glasgow pub the other night how it was going with him and his wife both being on a joint diet. "She's finding it heavy going," he replied, then added: "Put it this way. It'd probably be safer for me to go home smelling of perfume than her catching a whiff of a Mars bar from me."

CONGRATULATIONS to Jinty McGuinty's in Ashton Lane being named Pub of the Year in *Dram Magazine*'s Scottish Bar Awards. It actually is run by a Jinty - Jinty Lynch, whose father was a Ghanaian-born boxer from Maryhill if memory serves me right, although memory is usually a bit hazy after a night in Irish bar Jinty's. I do remember being there one night when a young woman, fed up with her friend going on about her latest dating disaster, rather tartly told her: "Oh for goodness sake, I've had showers that have lasted longer than some of your relationships."

A MOUNT Florida reader on the train into Glasgow hears two chaps discussing a young woman they work beside, with one opining: "OK she might be good-looking, but she's actually not a very nice person." His more star-struck pal replied: "If I was that beautiful, I wouldn't be that nice either."

LANCASTRIAN stand-up Dan Nightingale is appearing at Glasgow's Drygate tonight. A reader who saw him recently said that Dan was being all mushy about having a new girlfriend whom he thought could be the one. Dan explained how important she was to him: "First date, Pizza Express. I didn't even download a voucher, that's how much I liked her. That's how you know it's for keeps isn't it, when it's a two-for-one night and you're not applying for it."

A READER in a Glasgow pub at the weekend heard a young chap who had fallen out with his girlfriend tell his pals: "It's okay though. She says she's no longer mad at me." However one of his mates warned: "That's the same as when your dentist says, 'This won't hurt'."

AH the path of true love. A Glasgow reader heard a young woman discussing her engagement with her pals in a pub the other night when she told them: "I said I wasn't going to change my surname to his when we were married as it seems so old-fashioned."

"What did he say to that?" a pal wanted to know.

"He said an engagement ring was old-fashioned, but I didn't seem to mind taking that."

IT was reported last week that the number of fish in the sea has nearly halved since 1970. As Nikki Erskine commented: "As a single woman this does not surprise me one bit."

A READER swears to us that he heard a woman in a Glasgow bar the other night tell her pals: "I'm beginning to think my moral compass runs on solar power. It never seems to work after it gets dark."

NOPE, can't avoid his gaze. A colleague determinedly marches over to our desk and declares: "I once went on a date with a dolphin. We just clicked."

A READER in a Glasgow pub at the weekend heard a chap tell his pals that he had forgotten his wife's birthday. When his mates asked him what excuse he had come up with, he said he had tried: "How do you expect me to remember your birthday when you don't look any older?"

TODAY'S piece of whimsy comes from Malcolm Campbell, who says: "I had to leave my last girlfriend due to her obsession with counting. I often wonder what she is up to now."

IT takes a certain type of person to live in Glasgow's West End it seems. A reader confides to us: "Before I moved there, when folk asked if I was seeing someone, they wanted to know if I had a boyfriend. Now, when a friend in Hyndland asks the question, they are usually wondering if I go to a therapist."

RELATIONSHIPS continued. A reader hears a chap in a Glasgow pub at the weekend ask his pals: "Why is it, whenever she says, 'We need to talk' it's never about football or what pub to go to?"

OUR story about the chap forgetting his wife's birthday reminds Linda FitzGerald in Killin: "Some years ago my husband and I were going on holiday to Florida, via Iceland, with friends.

"At passport control in Reykjavik, as the immigration officer handed back our passports he said, 'happy birthday' to our friend. The look on her husband's face, who had forgotten in all the excitement of travelling, was priceless."

WE mentioned slow dances, and Jim Scott recalls: "When I worked in UG Glass in Shettleston we had a Swedish apprentice whom we took to the dancing. He was a bit shy and did not have great grasp of English, and asked what he should say to the girl he was dancing with. We said, 'Compliment her, say you like her perfume'. One of the girls later told us that he said she was 'stinking beautiful'."

THE big charity run Race for Life took place through Glasgow's city centre at the weekend. The runners were going past The Counting House pub at George Square where a female onlooker with a generous girth pointed out a thin runner in skin-tight Lycra and told her boyfriend: "I could look like that."

She is presumably still working out his punishment after he replied: "Aye. Only in one of these fairground mirrors."

WE asked for your slow dance stories, and as the lights go up, we leave you with a reader who tells us: "One of my school-mates at Kilmarnock Academy was brave enough to go to the Saturday night dancing at the Grand Hall.

Dancing with an older, but very attractive, partner, he realised he was becoming rather excited. Like a gentleman, he moved the lower half of his body slightly backwards only to be reassured, 'It's a' right, son, it'll no break'."

A READER phones to tell us: "Isn't it strange that the time you take to tidy up your house before a friend comes over is in inverse proportion to how much you value the friendship?"

RELATIONSHIPS explained in Glasgow pubs, continued. A reader tells us he heard a chap in one such pub tell his pals: "So the girlfriend out of the blue asked me if I thought it was pos-sible to love the one person for the rest of your life. Apparently my reply of, 'If I find the right person' was not the right answer."

WE'VE not been told any chat-up lines that people have over-heard for a while - perhaps Scottish men are getting wise to how bad they are.

However one reader in Edinburgh did hear a chap in a city centre bar the other week tell a young woman: "Did you know that men with good memories make excellent lovers? And that's not my biased opinion - I read it in an article on the 4th of February 2010 at 6.41pm."

FATHER'S Day yesterday and social media was awash with folk writing messages about their dads. We liked the more cynical chap who observed: "I might just say Happy Father's Day to my dad in person, instead of on social media which he doesn't use, and wouldn't see."

And TV presenter Richard Osman joked: "On this special day, don't forget to remind tourists about the signs on UK public toilets. M is for Mothers and F is for Fathers."

DATING is still a big issue these days, and a reader in Glasgow heard some women discussing where to meet a chap you are going on a date with for the first time. The question of coffee shop versus pub was being debated with one woman claiming: "Don't go to a coffee shop. He's still going to look unattractive after your fourth latte, unlike after your fourth prosecco."

DEAR oh dear. A reader was at his golf club in Ayrshire when he heard one of the more conservative members announce: "Whenever I see a woman driving a bus I smile and think about how far we, as a society, have come in equality.

"And then I wait for the next bus."

THE complicated world of dating, continued. A West End reader hears a woman in a Byres Road coffee shop defending herself with her friends who say she is too stand-offish when men talk to her. She came out with the memorable line: "I give every man I talk to the benefit of the doubt, in that I doubt whether there's any benefit in talking to them."

"I KNOW it got me into trouble," said the chap overheard in a Glasgow pub the other night. "But I couldn't resist it. My wife said she couldn't find her phone, so I asked her, 'Would you like me to call it?' When she said that would be great, I put down my newspaper, and shouted: 'Phone! Here boy!'"

IT could happen to anyone. A South Side reader tells us about a female friend going out with her pals to a local Italian restaurant.

He tells us: "She decided to walk home and called hubby to let him know. He, being gallant, said he'd walk down to meet her. He gets to the bottom of the road and sees his beloved in the distance. Then he decides, as you do, that he would just hide in the bushes and when she walks past, jump out and give her a fright. Hides in bushes. Jumps out. Not his missus."

A READER phones to tell us: "Whenever I bump into someone who says, 'Long time no see,' I just reply, 'I know. We're really not that good friends'."

OUR tale of the husband jumping out to scare his wife, only to find it was the wrong woman, reminds May Ryan in Perth of when she attended a church service in Arrochar, and it was so busy because of tourists that she and her husband had to sit in one row with their three daughters in the row behind. Says May: "During Mass, and what was meant to be a reassuring gesture, my husband reached back to contact his daughters, but unfortunately a lady arrived late and squeezed in beside them which made them move up the pew, and my husband found he was caressing the knees of a complete stranger."

12

Eating Out

Who doesn't like going out for a meal? There was a time when there were only a couple of posh restaurants in Glasgow, one or two Italians, and the rest of us had to make do with Wimpy. Now there are places to eat on every corner, throwing up, if that is the phrase, a story or two.

A PITHY, if sad, little notice spotted on the door of the now-empty La Tasca restaurant in Glasgow's Renfield Street. It records the venue's last day of trading, apologises for any inconvenience, and thanks the loyal customers who dined there over the years. It was however an expression near the end that caught our eye: "Shut happens", it says, followed by three smiley-face emojis.

A READER sends us a poster from America which claims to say what type of person you are depending on what type of coffee you drink. Under mocha it states in a very strange way: "You claim to have seen a ghost but it was actually a Scottish person sunbathing."

AND a woman at a Christmas lunch in Glasgow yesterday was heard to observe: "It's funny how eight glasses of water a day seems impossible, but eight glasses of wine can be done in one meal."

A PARTICK reader is feeling a bit down in the dumps after his family took him out to a West End restaurant to celebrate his 45th birthday. His wife sneaked a birthday cake to the staff for them to bring out after the meal and handed the waitress two candles shaped as "4" and a "5" to put on it. Our reader is crushed that the young waitress looked over at him, and then asked his wife what order the two numbers go on the cake.

FOOD snobs continued. Says Russell Smith in Kilbirnie: "Having a nice meal in a London restaurant some years ago my wife and I exchanged a small sample from our main dish and overheard a very polite English lady commenting, 'They must be Scottish - they're eating off each other's plates'."

THE Herald business story that haggis makers Macsween are to go back to their roots as a traditional butcher reminds John Bannerman in Kilmaurs: "In days of old, butchers and house-wives had a small hand-driven mincing machine fixed to the table. My mother-in-law had such an item, which was her pride and joy, as she was a great cook.

"Returning from the 'Rural' meeting one night, she was shocked to walk into the cottage to find her husband and his brother putting bars of thick black pipe tobacco through the machine. I never knew that a quiet wee woman could utter such words of condemnation."

A WAITER in the West End swears to us that he asked a girl

how her meal was and she pulled out her phone, looked at it, and told him: "Not good. It only got two likes on Instagram."

A READER tells us he was in a Glasgow pub at the weekend when a group of topers were discussing whether eating greasy pies was bad for your health. One of them eventually declared: "If eating pies takes three years off your life, I'd rather it was 1980 to 1983 when I made a real fool of myself."

WISE words spotted by David Donaldson on a board outside a West End coffee shop in Glasgow. Staff had written on it: "Three things that don't lie: 1. Kids. 2. Drunks. 3. Leggings."

WRITER Hugh McMillan has brought together a collection of irreverent stories about Dumfries and Galloway in the book just published by Luath Press, *McMillan's Galloway*.

In it he tells of the Dumfries local, famous for being an excellent fisherman who was notoriously poor at having permits for it, being asked in the pub if he could secure a large salmon for someone willing to pay him for it.

Writes Hugh: "He was expecting it the following weekend or something like that. Willie rubbed his grizzled chin and replied in his Galloway Irish lilt that it was a distinct possibility and could we just wait there? Within 10 minutes he was back with a giant salmon in a bin bag, headless and gutted.

"My friend paid him the money and Willie scarpered to one of his other haunts, leaving us to deal, ten minutes afterwards, with the chef of a nearby hotel who had been about to cook it for a wedding banquet when it had vanished from the kitchen table."

HUGH also mentions in the book our old journalistic chum Phil Mulvey, who sadly died in an accident in Vietnam a few years ago.

When Phil was working in Dumfries, says Hugh, "he had the job of editing a hugely respectful obituary of a local bigwig, notorious in the town for his drunkenness. Of course the paper was only meant to reflect the respectable side of his life but at the end instead of "sadly missed" Philip substituted "sadly pissed", claiming it to be an unfortunate typing error."

CHILDREN in restaurants, continued. Says Jim Thomson: "I went with my sons, aged about nine and six, to dinner, and to pass the time we played I Spy, with my younger son saying, 'Something beginning with, Ch'. We could not find the answer. Eventually the other people in the restaurant including the waiter all joined in with suggestions. At last, we all had to give in and there was a hush as Peter told us he was surprised we didn't get it. 'Tulips', he announced."

13
The Wiser Sex

Some stories about women show what strange, complicated, but clever and funny people they are.

WOMEN'S friends can be harsh critics. A reader in a busy Glasgow city centre pub at the weekend heard one woman tell her pal: "Why did you tell him you were 38? The last time you saw 38 was waiting for a bus to Shawlands."

A READER was in a Glasgow city centre pub at the weekend where he heard a woman sharing a bottle of wine with her pals announce expansively: "I'm my own worst critic." The moment was spoiled, he felt, by one pal piping up: "Trust me, you're not."

YOU can't beat a Glaswegian for a good insult. A reader on a bus into the city heard one young lady tell her pal: "Sophie came oot the tanning salon, and she had been in so long she had white rings roond her eyes from the goggles. She asked if it made her look like a clown. I said, 'Pit it this way Sophie, ah wouldnae be surprised if weans start askin' ye fur balloons'."

TELLY programmes about haunted houses were being discussed by women in a Glasgow coffee house when one declared: "I think my house is haunted. Every time I stand in front of a mirror, an old lady comes and stands in front of me and blocks my reflection."

THE Times newspaper has named Glasgow's Finnieston as the hippest place to live in Britain. It has certainly been livened up with bars and restaurants since the Hydro arena opened nearby. A reader once told us that he was in a bar in Finnieston when the peace and quiet was shattered by a gaggle of women arriving and demanding drink after attending a Michael Buble concert in the Hydro. They all wanted to be served at once so the under-pressure barman shouted out: "Right, let's do this the easy way. Oldest first."

Suddenly, says our reader, you could have heard a pin drop.

"DO you remember," said the woman in the Glasgow bar to her friends at the weekend, "that my New Year's resolution was to lose 10lbs this year?" She then clinked her wine glass with a pal's and added: "Only 15 more to go."

A READER swears to us that he heard a young woman in the West End being asked by her pals what she was doing that weekend, and she replied: "Oh just the usual - obsessing about problems that are only in my mind, then eating something I'll later regret."

14
Pets

We Scots are sentimental folk who love our pets. This is what they tell us about them.

NEWS from Australia where the state of New South Wales is banning greyhound racing from next year due to claims of cruelty. It reminds us of the reader who has a greyhound - they make great pets - who can't resist, when people stop him in the park and ask: "Have you ever raced it?", replying: "No, I'm not fit enough at my age."

TODAY'S piece of whimsy comes from Jake Lambert who asks: "Imagine if dogs found out that they are actually full of bones."

TALKING of pets, a reader phones us up to confess: "When I was young I worked at weekends in a pet shop. We had a tank with plants in it - but no animal - with a sign beside it proclaiming 'Chameleon'. People used to stand and stare at it for ages."

OUR pictures of angry, but funny, dog poo notices reminds John Crawford: "In East Ayrshire some communities wouldn't accept that bagged dog poo could be put in any litter bin (costing about £70) and petitioned their local councillors to have dedicated dog waste bins (costing about £175) instead. When a dog waste bin was damaged and had to be removed, people still left their wee bags of dog poo on the ground where the bin had been, obviously assuming the 'cooncil' would be along to collect it."

READER Bill Lothian muses: "In the pets section of my local Dobbies Garden Centre I came across a squeaky toy which claimed 'Only the dog can hear'. I've tried asking our dog if it works or is it a con trick, but can't get a response. Should I take the claim at face value?"

A CLARKSTON reader says the family has just got a new dog. He says it livens up the evening walks when someone stops and asks him what the dog's name is, and he replies: "He won't tell us."

A PIECE of whimsy from comedy writer Sanjeev Kohli, who declares: "If I'd have known my phone call would be 'recorded for training porpoises', I would have done a series of high-pitched clicks."

THE *Herald* farming story that reports of livestock worrying have increased by 55 per cent reminds Margery Dobson: "Years ago when I lived in Argyll, sheep were one of the main motoring hazards as fences were not a high priority for hill farmers.

"Each year at lambing time, a notice would appear in the *Oban Times* warning that any dog caught worrying sheep would be shot. Next to this would be a notice over the name of the editor announcing that any sheep found in his garden would be similarly treated."

TODAY'S piece of whimsy comes from Derek England in Erskine who says: "Friend of mine asked for some advice about how to start a dog collection. I said I'd give him a few pointers."

MARTIN McGeehan in Gourock couldn't believe it when he heard of someone throwing a birthday party for their dog. "What do you do?" he asks. "Break off a stick from a tree on the way there, give it to the dog, and wish it many happy returns?"

15
School

The best days of our lives? Let's see what the readers think.

WE mentioned teachers enjoying the summer break, and one Glasgow teacher swears to us that, when marking the last crop of homework before the break, she wrote in the top right corner of one essay jotter 'Date?' as she was fed up with pupils who forgot to write when the homework was done. She needed a holiday when one pupil wrote below it: "No thanks. I'm too young to be in a relationship."

SCHOOL holidays continued. A South Side reader tells us he was at the cinema in Silverburn when a woman arrived with a gaggle of noisy children.

She got the four of them seated in a row in front of our poor reader, and then she quietly walked away and sat in a different row.

WE asked how you were coping with the school holidays, and a Hillhead reader tells us: "My six-year-old walked into the room and said, 'Don't worry, dad. I'm okay'. I immediately knew it was time to search the house to find what he had broken."

ARGYLL reader Gerry Burke has used his free time to help pupils in his local primary school grow vegetables in a polytunnel. He tells us: "I was explaining the use of various forms of pest control to a group of pupils whose attention was focused on a large slug removed from the abundant lollo rosso lettuce crop.

"I was holding forth on the pros and cons of pesticides and herbicides when the dilemma was settled abruptly by a little foot descending on the creature. 'Sorted', she declared to the enthusiastic cheers of classmates who clearly had not been impressed by my David Attenborough impression."

DO schools still do nativity plays these days? Don't hear of them so often. A Glasgow reader remembers a few years ago getting the bus into town when the two women sitting in front were discussing the daughter of one of them appearing in the school play, and one asking: "What part is she playing?" The other woman replied: "She wanted to be Mary, but she ended up as one of the shepherds." After a pause she then lowered her voice and added: "It always comes down to who you know."

WE were feeling in a magnanimous mood as we said hello to a passing colleague who stopped to tell us: "I used to bury my head in the sand at school exam time. Eventually he expelled me."

MANY teenagers are sitting their Higher Prelims just now in Scotland, which reminds us of the constant debate as to what good learning algebra was all those years ago. As Craig Deeley puts it: "If I learnt anything in algebra lessons at school it was how to deflect sunlight off my watch on to the back of the maths teacher's head."

A READER swears to us that he was on the Underground in London when he heard a posh metropolitan woman complain about the difficulties her daughter was encountering at school. She told her friend: "The new class has filled with girls from Japan. Standards have unfairly risen."

SCHOOL proms are a growing phenomenon in Scotland - fancy parties for teenagers leaving school for the last time. A correspondent in Ayrshire tells us: "Since school proms caught hold here, it has become custom and practice for the various mums, aunties, and big sisters to go along to the hotel to watch the little dears arrive.

"The staff at one hotel saw something last week they have never seen before - when two of the pupils at one school brought along their babies, all dolled-up, to be in the prom pictures, before being handed over to granny and taken home."

BIG day today in Scotland's secondary schools, with the Higher English taking place. A teacher tells us she was once marking an essay where the pupil gave an account of a book he had read and how the plot fitted in with the question being asked. She had never heard of the book, and when she tried to find it on the internet, discovered no such book existed. She was impressed nevertheless that the pupil had invented an entire novel simply to answer the question.

A GLASGOW teacher is desperately wishing for the summer holidays after threatening a disruptive pupil that he would contact the child's parents to tell them of his behaviour. However when he loudly asked: "What would your mother say if I phoned her?", the class erupted when the lad in question replied: "Hello".

SCOTTISH schools are breaking up for the summer now. One relieved teacher heading for the pub tells us he received a note from an angry parent about their precious princess who was in his class which stated: "Please don't correct her spelling. It knocks her confidence."

16

A Shopper's Tale

It can be a stressful time, shopping. Sometimes humour can help relieve that stress.

A CLARKSTON reader has just finished a temporary job doing some market research for a supermarket chain.
She says she stopped one shopper and asked him: "How much do you spend on a bottle of wine?" The chap thought about it and replied: "About 20 minutes."

A SHAWLANDS reader was in a branch of Boots the chemist where he was asking for products to help folk stop snoring. The woman assistant came round to show him which aisle they were on, and she remarked there was less call for them these days. When our reader asked why, she replied: "I think most of the women have just left their snoring men." Warming to her theme she then added: "I've heard there's something new on the market - a mallet."

WE return to the product reviews on Amazon where folk occasionally have a bit of fun. Someone bought a Bic pen and wrote: "Worked fine with my right hand, but when I came to use my left hand my writing came out looking like the work of a complete imbecile. I can only assume Bic have created a right-handed only pen, and would caution left-handers to 'try before you buy'."

A READER swears to us he was in a Poundland store in Glasgow where he heard a woman shopper tell her pal: "Poundland must have really had some fantastic stuff back in the 1930s."

A NEWTON Mearns reader received a text from his wife yesterday which read: "Nothing to tell you, but just got back into my car at Silverburn, and some idiot in a BMW is angrily

waving at me to drive out so he can get my space. So thought I would send this first."

MANY folk were also shocked that it is now November, fearing that snow and Christmas shopping is just around the corner. A reader in Glasgow heard one chap remark: "Aye the first of November the day. Or as it's known in the supermarket trade, the backside has fallen out of the pumpkin trade so knock them out for a quid day."

SHOULD we believe the student who works part-time in Waitrose in Glasgow's West End who told his pals that a customer came over and told him she was looking for Oregano and Guava. He tried to give her directions to the correct aisles when she explained she had lost sight of her young children.

A READER who deplores graffiti, spots on the wall of the toilet cubicle at Waterstone's bookshop in Edinburgh's Princes Street, that someone had written: "You'd think a bookshop would have something to read in here."
Quite logically someone had added below it: "I guess they do now."

AH, the start of Christmas shopping. Glasgow stand-up Janey Godley tells us: "I had a small stab of sympathy for the 50+ man with dark dyed hair, orange trench-coat, bright jeans, and tired face out shopping with his blonde younger second wife.

He was being dragged round perfume counters with his wife getting annoyed at him for moaning that he did all this back in the 80s with his first wife."

A READER getting the train into Glasgow heard a young man who was flicking through his mobile phone tell his pals: "Half the contacts in my phone deliver food."

THE news that Irn-Bru is no longer putting deposits on their glass bottles reminds a reader: "I was turning from Cambridge Street into Sauchiehall Street in Glasgow city centre when I noticed two carrier bags with about ten empty Irn-Bru bottles next to a bin. As soon as I turned the corner there was a guy, worse for wear, asking for 'change for a wee cup of tea'.

 "I pointed out to him the Irn-Bru bottles and told him they were worth £3. His reply? 'You're a miserable b******'. It's degrading to take them to the shop!'"

READERS often reminisce about things we no longer have that we miss. There is one we had never thought of until William Ader commented: "I miss not being able to put things on top of the TV."

A GLASGOW reader says he thought he was being funny when he went to the hairdresser's, and when the girl asked what he wanted, he replied: "Make me look attractive to women." The girl topped his gag however by shouting to an imaginary colleague in the back shop: "Linda! Cancel the rest of my appointments for today."

MINTS continued. Says Ron Hanvey: "I was stationed in Glasgow during my National Service alongside an English sergeant major who directed a private to buy him a quarter pound bag of mints. On arriving back hotfoot, the private proudly presented him with a neatly tied little bag. On opening it, the sergeant major fiercely demanded an explanation why he had been presented with a very tiny amount of mince."

GET anything useful in the sales? A Glasgow reader was in one emporium where fridges were being sold at a discount. He heard one young man, after opening a fridge door and staring at the lay-out, comment to the young woman with him: "Clearly the people that design refrigerators don't know me if they think one tiny cheese drawer and two giant vegetable drawers are a reflection of my eating habits."

"WHY is it," mused a Newton Mearns reader, "that we can't donate old clothes to a charity shop without driving around with them in the boot of the car for at least six months?"

GREAT to see vinyl making a slow but steady comeback in the music industry. A reader was in a vintage record store when a fellow browser asked how much an album was. The chap behind the counter said: "That one's £7. But there's a surcharge if I have to listen to your story about how your mother or your wife made you throw out your old vinyl collection."

ROBIN Gilmour in Milngavie was in a supermarket when a chap was stopped from buying multiple packets of paracetamol. When he questioned the assistant said it was in case someone was wanting to kill themselves.

The chap pointed at the packet of soap powder he was also buying and argued: "If ah wanted to kill masel, ah widnae waste ma money buyin' soap powder, would ah?"

A READER was in a Glasgow branch of a large DIY store when a chap staggered up to the check-out with a big paving stone with no label on it that could be scanned.

After staring at it dubiously the woman at the checkout told him she didn't think the store sold them.

The puffing customer replied: "No, you're right. I found it outside and thought I'd bring it in to show you!"

THE news that Tesco is selling Dobbies Garden Centres reminds us of the Edinburgh woman who was heard telling her husband in Dobbies that they should take the pest control firm leaflet in order to get rid of the mole in their garden. However her husband remonstrated: "We're not killing the mole. We live in our house, and the mole's house is the garden. I mean, how would you like it if the mole tried to get in and kill us?" His wife replied: "Oh, don't be silly!" Then added after a pause: "It couldn't, could it?"

ENJOY the bank holiday yesterday? A reader thought it was a tad harsh of the woman shopper who loudly remarked in a south side shopping centre: "Is today actually Bring Your Crying Wean to Silverburn Day?"

THE Bank of Scotland branch in Clarkston Road in Muirend has closed down. Gerry Mann tells us that someone has gone to the bother of printing out an additional notice, taped below the one which says, "The branch has now closed", with the second one stating: "Please form an orderly queue at that door and we're confident you'll notice very little difference in service."

We assume it's not an official Bank of Scotland notice.

BEING asked by a woman what you think of a potential purchase - never a wise idea. Reader Peter McMahon heard a woman trying on a hat for a wedding ask her presumably bored husband what he thought of the umpteenth hat she had tried on. "It's a good multipurpose one," he replied. When she asked what he meant he told her: "After wearing it at the wedding it could also double as a wreath at a funeral."

A HILLHEAD reader swears to us that she saw a friend buying a pregnancy testing kit in the local chemist. When her pal turned round and saw her, she said: "Nothing to worry about. When I'm having a really bad day I like to take a pregnancy test to remind myself that things could be much worse."

BIG problems for Scotland's transport with the news that the Forth Road Bridge is to be closed for weeks. Nevertheless some folk have been making fun about the plight of Fife being set adrift from civilisation. But as one canny local put on social media: "To all you Edinburgh citizens laughing at Fifers being cut off from you - the Amazon warehouse is on our side. Merry Christmas."

17

Out and About

Thank goodness folk still use public transport to work as the Diary would be a poorer place without their stories.

A READER was on a bus in the west end when a young woman came on with her two children, sat them down, and told them: "If you behave yourselves, you can both get a rice cake."

"Wouldn't work in my day," the pensioner behind them muttered.

NEWS from north of the Central Belt, and Bruce Skivington reveals: "There was a reporter out in the wilds asking if the new speed cameras on the A9 had made a difference. The local he was speaking to said it took 10 minutes longer. The reporter asked if that was because people were driving slower. 'No,' replied the local. 'That's how long it takes to tie a bit of cardboard over the number plate.'"

FOR some reason we stumbled into Ayrshire bus stories, and Carol Johnston tells us: "I was on the Cumnock to Ayr bus recently when a man with a huge scar across his head, held together with staples, stumbled on and told everyone, 'See this? An ex did this!' Someone replied, 'Aw man, that's pure terrible. She must have been a right wan!' After a puzzled silence the man burst out laughing and said, 'Naw! Ma pal hit me on the heid wae an ex!' as his local accent for a sharp implement perhaps confused some passengers."

THE tunnel out of Glasgow's Queen Street Station's upper level has shut for five months, which will lead to lengthier train journeys. It reminds us of the West End reader who was taking her bicycle on the train to Stirling and asked for a return ticket. "Why don't I just give you a single," said the ticket seller trying to be encouraging. "It's only 20 miles. You could manage that."

YOU get some memorable conversations waiting for a bus in Glasgow. Says Mary Duncan: "I recently was at a bus stop in the

East End, bus pass at the ready, when an elderly chap, perhaps a wee bit the worse for drink, said to me, 'Is that you using' yer mother's bus pass?' When I turned to get on the bus, he turned to his pal and said, 'Ah'll need tae get some new chat-up lines'."

IAN Power, we suspect, speaks for many when he declares: "As well as full and provisional licences I'm beginning to suspect there's a 'no test needed just as long as you only do the school run' one."

AN unsettling piece of graffiti was seen by a reader at her local bus stop where someone had scrawled: "Are you SURE you switched the iron off?"

A PAISLEY reader says he has just bought a house which is nearer Glasgow Airport, and the pros and cons of such a move were being discussed by his friends. Handy to get away on your holidays but likely to be noisy being the two main arguments. However, he thought one pal was a genius for suggesting: "You could of course confuse thousands of people by painting 'Welcome to Edinburgh' on your roof."

PROVERBS being updated due to recent news events - "Where there's smoke there's a VW Polo."

TALKING of trains, and how busy they are between Glasgow and Edinburgh just now. A reader phones to suggest: "If someone gets on, looks at the seat beside you, and asks, 'Is there anyone sitting there?' grab them by the arm, looking intensely in their eyes, and whisper, 'So you can see them too, can you?'"

YOU need to know your buses in Glasgow. A reader was on a bus going to Braehead from the city centre, but some folk were taken unawares when it veered off the route to take a detour to the new hospital on the south side.

"If ah'd knew it wis gonnae take this long," declared the wee wummin behind, "Ah'd a brung ma flask!"

"ENJOYING the Indian summer?" said the pensioner wearing a T-shirt getting on a bus on Glasgow's south side and spotting an old pal on board.

"Better than Indians would enjoy a Scottish winter," his old chum replied.

TOM Rafferty tells us of a friend travelling on the train from Glasgow to Aberdeen. Says Tom: "The chap sitting next to her wanted to buy his ticket with a debit card, and when he held it up, the ticket seller remarked, 'Oh TSB? Dodgy.'

"The traveller acknowledged that if the ticket seller meant they were partly responsible for the crash of the economy then they were indeed dodgy. But the ticket seller replied, 'No, I meant they don't work in my machine'."

OUR story about Americans reminds Kate Woods: "I was on the ferry from Gourock to Dunoon on a pouring wet winter's night when the American submarine base at the Holy Loch was still operating.

As we lined up on deck in the lashing sleet to get off the boat, a wee wummin slipped beside a very tall American wearing a huge Stetson and said, 'D'you mind if I stand under your hat son?'"

ROBERT Gardner tells us that on one plane out of Glasgow recently, the head steward came on and apologised for a mix-up in catering, and the flight had only been delivered 40 dinners, so if anyone was willing to give up having a meal they would be given some complimentary drinks.

Robert says that half an hour later the steward came back on to say that surely there were 40 folk on board who wanted to have a meal.

OUR story about the drunk on board the mobile art gallery bus reminds John Henderson: "During a Paisley by-election Labour had a campaigning double decker bus which we parked outside a bingo hall one afternoon, and as the hall started to empty, we invited people to step on board for the campaign spiel and a poster.

"Snag was these wee Paisley wifies just sat down, believing it was a free bus home put on by the bingo hall.

"It was much easier just asking them to tell us where to let them off as we toured the scheme, as I didn't have the heart to tell them it was a campaign bus for the Labour Party."

OUR tales about CalMac ferries remind reader Bob Byiers: "My favourite concerns an American tourist family driving on to a west coast pier just in time to see the ferry sail away. The father accosts the official on the pier, 'Gee man! We've come all the way from Chicago to catch that ferry!' to which the McBrayne's man replies, 'Well if you'd left Chicago 10 minutes earlier, you would've caught it'."

YES, we waited for a bus story, and three came along at once. Alastair Cherry tells us: "Trinity College Choir, made up of the theological students at Glasgow University, was perform-ing in Edinburgh one year, and one of the students had an old MacBrayne's bus collect us and take us to the concert. One night, as he waited for us to board, a gentleman got on the bus and sitting himself down congratulated the driver on MacBraynes restoring the Oban service again. He was disappointed when told we were only bound for Morningside that night."

SOME banter just deserves to be repeated. Says Mungo Henning: "Overheard on a train down from Glasgow to Ayrshire from a young woman to her glum-looking beau, 'Gie yur face a biscuit'."

And on a bus into Glasgow, a reader heard an overly made-up young girl ask her boyfriend: "So on a scale of nine and a half to ten, how gorgeous am I?"

A SOUTH side reader swears he heard a young woman on the train the other day tell her pal: "I had to get my blood tested. Apparently I got a B plus. I'm hoping for an A next time."

FERRY operators CalMac has a new advertising campaign called "Eejits" where two lads, perhaps not the brightest, go touring in the Scottish islands. Says reader Foster Evans: "It does remind me of the late Whiteinch housing chief John Ross watching a drunk being refused black coffee on the trip from Ullapool to Stornoway. When the drunk eventually fell asleep John asked why he had been refused the coffee. He was told: 'There is nothing worse than a waking drunk'."

STILL shocking weather out there. Reader John Mulholland recalls: "I was once waiting for a train at Edinburgh's Haymarket during the evening rush hour when snow and the elements were causing chaos with the train timetable. There were so many cancellations and platform changes that passengers were becoming increasingly frustrated. The stationmaster lightened the mood by announcing, 'For passengers on platform four, please note we are having weather problems. That is whether or not the next train to arrive will be for Dunblane or Glasgow, or whether one arrives at all'."

18
Health

It's no laughing matter not being well - but then again it can be according to our readers.

ANNIE McQuiston tells us about a doctor pal who has a coffee mug he uses at work which many medical staff will probably want. We think it is for his patients to read. On the mug is printed: "Please do not confuse your Google search with my medical degree".

A PIECE of sheer whimsy from Moose Allain who tells us: "I narrowly avoided being beaten up by a gang smoking e-cigarettes last night. I nearly had an attack of the vapers!"

Incidentally we heard a chap tell his pals he saw an inebriated woman in Glasgow outside a pub trying to light her e-cigarette, which is not a good look.

Unfortunately during meal service the balcony is a non-smoking area.

We apologise for your slightly extended lifespan.

WAITING in the local accident and emergency department, a Borders reader watches a couple come in with the husband nursing a hand injury. He feels the chap must have done something stupid as when his wife was giving details to the receptionist about what happened, she added: "And put on the form, 'Do Not Resuscitate'."

WE mentioned Glasgow rhyming slang, and Tom Morrice tells of a colleague who went to the doctor complaining of sore legs and the doctor asked him if he had any varicose veins.

"Yes," he replied, "a boy and a girl."

DONNIE Pollock in Glasgow reads the label on some medicine to control overactive bladders, and he muses: "Got to hand it to the manufacturers. 'Take with water', it says on the box. Now that's confidence for you."

COULDN'T help it, but I knew the office joker had been in hospital so I felt I had to go up and ask him how he was. He immediately recounted: "When I came round, the surgeon told me he had just messed up my operation. My heart was in my mouth."

GARY Delaney remarks: "Botox can't be that expensive. When users are given the bill they don't look surprised."

DIFFICULT to know what to eat and what not to eat with all these health scares surrounding sugar, fat, saturates and goodness knows what else. A reader tries to simplify it for us by stating: "The key to eating healthy is avoiding any food that has a TV commercial."

"I NEED that pint," said the toper in the Glasgow pub at the weekend. "I fell aff a 15ft ladder this morning." His pals quickly got him the pint before he added: "I was only on the bottom rung. But still."

WE overheard a chap having a coffee at the Emirates sports stadium yesterday tell his pal: "I've got to get into shape. Do you know, if I was murdered right now my chalk outline would be a circle."

ALAN Barlow in Paisley was picking up his prescription from the chemist, and the antibiotics he was being given carried the instruction that alcohol should not be taken while on the course of treatment. Says Alan: "On receiving my pills I was about to leave when the chemist said in a very loud voice, 'remember - no alcohol'. This earned me a thumbs up and a 'you can do it big man' from a member of the queue waiting for his methadone."

KEEPING fit is a huge industry these days. But not everyone is a convert. A reader heard a customer in a Glasgow boozer at the weekend declare: "So if you eat what you like, and don't exercise, eventually you get a motorised scooter. I'm really not seeing the downside to all this."

OH my goodness, friends can be a bit sarky, can't they? A Glasgow reader was in town at the sales yesterday when she heard a young woman tell her pal: "I'm thinking of buying a treadmill. Do you think they'll let me try it out first?" "What are you going to do?" replied her pal, "Ask them if you can bring your laundry in and hang damp clothes over it?"

BRIAN Chrystal reads the news story that the new Queen Elizabeth Hospital in Glasgow has had operations disrupted because of "raw sewage" coming though the ceiling and he wonders: "Would cooking it first make it any better, though?"

OTHER news stories at the weekend were the odds of 45 million to one of winning the big lottery jackpot, and the suggestion from the Chief Medical Officer that all alcohol is bad for you. A Glasgow reader combines both stories by pointing out: "The lottery gives you a 45,000,000 to 1 chance that you won't go to work tomorrow. Alcohol gives you a one in five chance."

19

Off On Your Holidays

We usually do get a laugh when we go on holiday, even if the weather is not the best.

WE are in the Glasgow Fair holiday fortnight just now, but of course it is no longer as memorable as it used to be. We recall when Blackpool was inundated with Glaswegians at the Fair, and a reader told us he was outside a Gypsy Rose Lee fortune-telling

booth on Blackpool's Golden Mile when he heard a Glaswegian, who'd had a few drinks, loudly ask: "Don't tell me any o'
that relationship rubbish. I just want tae know - whit hotel am
I stayin' in?"

A FEW readers are just returning from late summer holidays,
and a south-side reader tells us about being at St Mark's Square
in Venice when he heard a Scottish voice at a nearby table que-
rying the rather large bill for two coffees. The waiter explained
to him that there was a sizeable surcharge for the musicians
playing in the background. "If I'd known," replied the Scotsman
loudly, "that I was going to be paying for the music I'd have
listened to it."

WE FEEL the pain of Glasgow stand-up Janey Godley, en route
to compering a charity show in Spain, who told us on social
media yesterday: "There is a man in the queue for the Malaga
flight drinking a pint of lager. It's like 1978." Minutes later, once
on board she added: "The easyJet guy just announced over the
Tannoy, 'We have run out of Stella'. It hasn't even taken off
yet!"

A READER flying back to Glasgow from a hot and sunny
holiday in Portugal tells us that there was a collective groan
in the cabin when the chief steward announced that they
would shortly be landing, and that the weather in Glasgow
was rain. Hearing the negative comments the steward then

added: "Oh come on, it's Glasgow, not Barbados. What were you expecting?"

CONVERSATIONS that just have to be passed on. Chris Fyfe tells us: "Was passing the bike-hire shop in Millport yesterday and heard a lassie tell her pal, 'Ah don't know if ah want to cycle all the way roon the island.' So her pal suggested, 'Why do ye no just go half way and then cycle back?'"

MUSIC fan Mike Ritchie tells us: "Have just returned from the absolutely wonderful Kilkenny Roots Festival in the Republic of Ireland. My B&B was a mile out of town, and in an adjoining field there was a friendly grey mare. As I was leaving, my host said, 'I'm glad you like the horse so I've got something for you to take with you.' How kind, I thought. He then handed me two slices of bread and said, 'Could you feed these to it on your way down the driveway?'"

ENJOY the Easter weekend? A reader sums it up: "Wake up full of joy at the prospect of an extra long weekend. Spend the day on your couch watching any old rubbish on the telly. At around 8pm feel gripped by acute sadness that you've wasted the entire day and have to go back to work tomorrow."

GOT your holidays booked yet? A flight attendant working out of Glasgow Airport swears to us that a woman asked if she could change her seat as she couldn't stand sitting next to a crying child. The stewardess checked, and discovered it was the woman's child.

ONE of Scotland's new tourist successes is the growing number of cruise ships now docking at Greenock, from where the cruisers are taken on coach tours of the west of Scotland. John Duthie tells us a group of visitors had arrived on the ship, the Disney Magic, the other day, and the driver of the coach they were on announced to the passengers as they drove along that he and his wife were once in a Disney shop in Florida.

"What are you wanting?" he asked his wife. "Disnae matter," she told him as she was not after anything in particular. But the shop assistant who was hovering immediately told them: "We don't have a Disney Matter."

PACKING for your holidays? An Ayrshire reader tells us a member at his golf club posed the question: "Why is it I wear one shirt a day, every day, all my life, yet when we go on holiday for a week my wife insists on packing 21 shirts for me?"

SCOTT Ritchie tells us: "Your story of the mother not wanting to sit next to her noisy child on a plane reminds me of a stewardess who moved a lady passenger to a new seat to get her away from a drunk sitting beside her on a flight from Spain to Glasgow. As the plane approached Glasgow Airport, the stewardess asked if the lady wanted to return to her original seat for landing. 'Oh, I suppose I had better go back and sit beside my husband' was the reply."

A GLASGOW family on holiday in Harris and Lewis last week was visiting St Clement's Church at Rodel, a 16th century church and a bit of a tourist attraction. They went into the ancient building, the door creaking loudly and smelling of centuries of worship. There they found a chap irately telling his young son: "No, I'm telling you, they definitely won't have Wi-Fi here."

20

Gone But Not Forgotten

It's been a shocking year for the loss of some great people. Our readers tell us their fond memories.

THE death of Muhammad Ali reminds us of when the late boxing promoter Mickey Duff brought the great boxer to Paisley ice rink for an exhibition bout. The story was told that at a dinner in Glasgow Ali was introduced to Rangers footballer Willie Henderson, and seeing Willie's weather-worn visage, Ali asked him what he did for a living, and when Willie told him, Ali replied: "Football! I'm glad I stuck to boxing."

SAD to hear of the death of Glasgow-based author Margaret Thomson Davis. She once explained that when writing she would become engrossed in the lives of her characters. She was writing about a sex-obsessed Bearsden woman at a time when she had to give a speech in front of Glasgow's Lord Provost and other dignitaries. Without thinking, she peppered her speech with risqué jokes, including the one about the minister who discovered one of his flock was working as a prostitute.

Shocked and upset, he met her next day and told her that he had prayed for her the previous night.

She replied: "Oh you didn't need to do that - I'm on the phone."

Recalled Margaret: "Nobody laughed, except the Lord Provost, who was immediately silenced by his wife."

WE wrote about the death of comedy writer Victoria Wood, and a reader sends us her favourite gag by Victoria. "My boyfriend had a sex manual but he was dyslexic. I was lying there, and he was looking for my vinegar."

SAD to hear of the death of former Fire Brigades Union general secretary Ken Cameron who originally hailed from Fort William. He once told me that he had got a job as a trainee reporter when he left school with the Aberdeen *Press and Journal* and was sent to write about an international swimming gala.

Unfortunately, the press were put in the front row, and as he left his seat he tried to get round a fellow attendee who was standing in front of him. Both moved in the same direction, and young Ken ended up in the pool, disrupting the contest.

Unfortunately, a rival newspaper wrote about it, and Ken's journalistic career was terminated - possibly one of the few journalists to make a splash rather than write one.

INCIDENTALLY, we also remember Ken attending the TUC annual conference in Blackpool, and realising the shop he had popped into was called Cameron Stores, he cheerily asked the owner whereabouts in Scotland his family came from, and wondering whether they were related. Instead all he got was a blank look.

It was only when he left the store that Ken noticed it was in fact situated in Cameron Road.

THE obituary in *The Herald* of Scots actor Alan Young explained that apart from appearing in the American TV series *Mr Ed*, he was also the voice of Disney character Scrooge McDuck, who, in one episode, revealed he had gone to America from Glasgow as a cabin boy before making his fortune. This story of Scrooge's origins is in fact confirmed by Glasgow City Council. On the council's website, under "Famous Glaswegians" the name Scrooge McDuck, described as "the richest duck in the world" is included.

COMEDIAN Ronnie Corbett's death reminds us of the story told of when he met his future comedy partner Ronnie Barker. Mr C was between jobs, working as a barman in a London club used by actors.

Because of his lack of inches there were two crates behind the bar, which he stood on, one with the name Agnes and the other with the name Champ.

It was only when Barker asked him who Agnes was that Corbett explained it was a crate marked Champagnes that had been sawn in half.

THE death of actor Warren Mitchell reminds writer Ian Pattison: "He was once doing his Alf Garnett show in London's West End, where the house was gratifyingly full - apart from two conspicuously empty seats in the middle of the front row. Mitchell was well into his performance when he was thrown by an elderly man and woman clomping down the centre aisle, disrupting the whole front row to take the empty seats. Mitchell chose to harangue the pair in his Alf guise. 'Look at the bleedin' time,' he rasped, 'I've been on for 30 minutes!' The old man looked up, saying, 'Yes, that's why we're late - we'd heard the first half hour wasn't very good'."

THE death of veteran ex-Tory Minister Geoffrey Howe reminds former Ayrshire Labour MP Brian Donohoe: "I will always remember the time he came campaigning in Irvine. He introduced himself to an Irvine worthy as, 'Hello I'm Geoffrey Howe'. The Irvine worthy replied, 'Who?' and Geoffrey slickly replied, 'No, Howe'."

SAD to hear of the untimely death of Dundee United star Ralph Milne. We remember in his autobiography that he wrote about the fines mercurial manager Jim McLean used to slap on his players for various infringements - with Ralph being one of the worst offenders. When the club had one of their best seasons ever, and won the Premier League in the 1980s, Ralph shouted out in the dressing room: "Hey, boss, see now that we've won the league, any chance I can get all my fines back? I've seen a house in the Ferry that I want to pay cash for."

His teammates were in fits. McLean's reply cannot be repeated in a family newspaper.

SUCH sad news that Scots author William McIlvanney has died. It wasn't so long ago that Willie was telling an audience at the Glasgow Film Theatre that he got one of his few negative reviews when he was walking down the road in Glasgow and "a big guy walking down the other side shouted, 'McIlvanney, who told you you could effin' write?' And I shouted back, 'Probably the same person who told you you could effin' read', and I hastened on, because he was a large fellow."

APART from being a beautiful writer, McIlvanney liked nothing better than telling a good story. He once recounted how he met Sean Connery at a Scotland match at Hampden. "I can't believe I'm here," Connery told him. "I was sitting in Tramp's at two o'clock this morning when Rod Stewart walks in. He's chartered a plane and why don't I come to the game? So here I am." Tramp's of course being a London nightclub.

A policeman with McIlvanney chipped in: "It's a small world, big yin. Ah was in a house in Muirhouse at two o'clock this morning. It was full o' tramps as well."

WE mentioned the sad death of inspirational Scots writer William McIlvanney, and we recall when he reviewed television for *The Herald*. Being Willie he would wander off into stories of whatever came to mind. As he told Herald readers after watching a David Attenborough wildlife programme: "After the last England-Scotland match at Wembley, a friend of mine finished late on Saturday night sitting thoughtfully drunk on the wall outside David Attenborough's house in Richmond, without any specific idea of where he was, when the police arrived to move him.

"Apparently Mr Attenborough had phoned for their assistance. Silverbacked gorillas are one thing. But only fools tackle drunk Scottish supporters.

"On being asked why he was outside David Attenborough's house, my friend had the presence of mind to reply, 'Somebody called me an animal. And I came for a second opinion'."

BOXING promoter Alex Morrison phones us to say: "Was just reading fellow boxing manager Jim Murray's obituary in *The Herald*. Jim was a friend of mine for years. He always joked, that as a strict vegetarian, he hoped for a big turnip at his funeral."

DAVID Bowie's death has shocked music fans everywhere. In Ayrshire, Matt Vallance tells us: "Bowie's passing reminds me of one of the great legends of Ayrshire music.

"Supposedly, back when he had just changed his name from David Jones to David Bowie, and he was touring small gigs in Scotland, Bowie and his band were booked to play Auchinleck Working Men's Club.

"The legend has it, when they were preparing to go on-stage, the Bowie band were asked if they could back another of the acts that night - a wee local who was a dab hand on the spoons. Whether they did or not is still a matter for debate."

THE Hidden Glasgow forum contains an old post from Dicky Hart, who used to work in the Barrowland Ballroom as gig

security. Lemmy, he wrote, asked for one of the fruit machines to be brought into his dressing room. He put a small fortune into it. As showtime neared, he warned everyone not to touch it as he was due some nudges.

LOTS of newspapers have been publishing readers' encounters with recently deceased music star David Bowie - gosh we've been doing it ourselves in the Diary. But prize for the most tenuous recollection must go to the *Croydon Advertiser*, which this week reported: "The Coulsdon man who delivered David Bowie's milk during the summer of '69 remembers the music legend as a 'nice man' who 'had time for people'."

AND chef Andy Cumming recalls: "My experience of David Bowie goes back to the 90s when he came to Glasgow to visit the David Hockney exhibition. He came into the Brasserie on West Regent Street for lunch with his family. I had just started a new menu and was unsure of one dish, perhaps a bit advanced for the Glasgow palate - squid ink linguine with feta cheese and sun-blushed tomatoes.

"Bowie ordered it and said it was fantastic. But yes, it was too advanced for Glasgow."

"I took it off the menu the next week."

SAD to hear of the death of Eagles guitarist Glenn Frey who became a passionate golfer and would always play in Scotland whenever the band came here. He was once asked why he waited years to take up golf, and he replied: "I waited for the clothes to get better."

However golfers who are always suspicious of other golfers' sizeable handicaps will sympathise with fellow rocker Alice Cooper who was beaten in a pro-am tournament by Glenn.

Remarked Cooper: "Glenn was playing with a handicap of 17. Either the 1 is wrong, or the 7 is wrong, but one of these numbers shouldn't be there."

OUR reference to the death of former Tory Minister Lord Parkinson reminds Bobby Buirds, a retired official with the then electricians' union, the EETPU: "Just after the Piper Alpha Disaster Cecil Parkinson, then Minister for Energy, asked to meet a survivor. Our President, and the worker, met him, and

Cecil Parkinson asked about the bandages on his head. The survivor said his head was badly burned and he was getting skin grafts taken from his backside.

"He then leaned across the desk and said, 'Well Minister, now you can kiss my arse' and patted his head.

THE death of former First Lady Nancy Reagan reminds us of when she and hubby were in Scotland at a dinner when Ronald was given the ceremonial title of Keeper of the Quaich by a whisky organisation. Much like at a Burns Supper, the haggis at the banquet was being addressed by a theatrical chap with a booming voice, and under the spotlights you could see the water spraying from his lips. "What happens next?" Nancy asked Lord Elgin sitting next to her. "We eat it," he said. To which an astonished Nancy said: "No way." And, indeed, no haggis left her plate.

FOOTBALL fans are still mourning the death of legendary player Johan Cruyff. Andy Bollen tells us: "Questions were asked about his seemingly peculiar choice of Scotland as a pre-season destination. Why would he bring his Barca superstars here? He could go anywhere, but Cruyff seemed to love the chilling cold wind and pelting rain of a Scottish summer. He was particularly fond of playing pre-season games against Dundee United and sharing their training facilities.

"Dundee United's training base just happened to be in St Andrews University, allowing JC the chance to play the Old Course all week while his players got fit. Genius."

MANY newspapers described record producer George Martin, who has died at the age of 90, as "the fifth Beatle". Our popular music expert explains: "Newspapers over the years have described former Beatles business manager Neil Aspinall, their main manager Brian Epstein, former band members Pete Best and Stuart Sutcliffe, and even footballer George Best as 'the fifth Beatle'. So that makes 10 Beatles in all. Glad to clear that up."

READER Ian Barnett once played a round of golf with Ronnie Corbett, who was of course a mad keen golfer. In his memory, Ian passes on his favourite of Corbett's many golf stories: "For some time, my wife's had this ridiculous idea that I'm playing too much golf. Actually, it came to a head at about 11.30 last night. She suddenly shouted at me: 'Golf, golf, golf. All you ever think about is bloody golf!' And I'll be honest, it frightened the life out of me. I mean, you don't expect to meet somebody on the 14th green at that time of night."

WE mentioned the posthumous autobiography of legendary *Sunday Post* editor Bill Anderson entitled *God Bless Mrs McGinty!* In it Bill talks about his National Service as an officer in Hong Kong when a Chinese chap carrying pots and pans wearily climbed to the top of the hill where Bill was stationed and pleaded for a job as a cook.

"Me have very very good reference" he declared and handed

Bill a worn page from an Army message-pad on which was written: "This is the worst ******* cook in the world."

Bill told him he had no job for him, but at least threw the reference in the stove and wrote him a new one which stated, "This is the best cook in the colony" and sent him on his way.

> **CORRECTION**
> The China Seafood Restaurant ad that ran in last Saturday's Green Section was incorrect. It read 中國鮮辭海至 . It should have read 店飯鮮海國中 . We regret any inconvenience this may have caused.

WE mentioned the sad death of Scots trade union leader Ken Cameron, former general secretary of the Fire Brigades Union, whose funeral was this week. Ken was a great supporter of many political causes, and colleague John McGhee recalled leaving a Scottish FBU meeting in Glasgow when they were crossing St Enoch's Square just as a small fascist rally was being filmed for an episode of *Taggart*. Ken, not realising it was actors, heard the rightwing slogans being shouted, and immediately veered across the square to remonstrate with the protesters.

SAD to hear of the death of poverty campaigner Bob Holman, who spent years in Easterhouse supporting community projects.

As he once recalled: "One evening in Easterhouse, I had driven into another neighbourhood to collect some jumble. A crowd of teenagers began to rock the minibus to tip it over with me inside.

"Then one shouted, 'Wait a minute. That's old Bob, he used to teach me table tennis'. They then held a whip-round for the jumble sale. Saved by table tennis."

SAD to hear of the death of Irish guitarist Henry McCullough who led a very rock 'n' roll life. An odd story about Henry is that he was at the Abbey Road studios, recording tracks with Paul McCartney's post-Beatles band Wings. In the studio next door Pink Floyd were recording *Dark Side of the Moon*. Someone was talking to Henry and he came out with the line: "I don't know - I was really drunk at the time." It was caught on tape on the Pink Floyd album and they liked the line so much they left it on the album.

21

Just Jokes and Stuff

Some of our stories are hard to categorise, and also a mention for my colleagues who feel the need to tell me their jokes. Here are the best, or is that worst?

I RECOGNISE the purposeful stride of a colleague, which means he wants to tell me something. So I wait. "Just met an illegal organs dealer," he bellows.

"Now there's a man after my own heart."

TOO late! A colleague catches our eye and comes over to tell us: "My parents said that if I was to get a tattoo I should get it done in a place that doesn't really matter and is out of sight.

"So I had it done in Bellshill."

MEANWHILE over at the Edinburgh Fringe, Mark Simmons at the Pleasance Courtyard reminds us that summer is over by remarking: "I've never had a tan - I think my sun cream's a huge factor."

TODAY'S piece of whimsy comes from Gary Delaney who says: "Some people get so tetchy about me reading over their shoulder. It's not even as if I'm that loud."

MANAGING any gardening between the rain? A reader asks us: "How do people in films dig six-foot graves with a shovel, when I get knackered just digging a hole to plant a bush?"

NORMALLY we eschew light bulb jokes, but having seen so many advertisements on the telly, we pass on: "How many personal injury lawyers does it take to screw in a light bulb?"
   "Three."
   "One to change the bulb, one to shake him off the ladder, and one to sue the ladder company."

JUST when I thought a colleague had gone off on holiday, he creeps up behind me and announces: "Did you know that I was banned from the Eskimo lottery? It seems you have to be Inuit to win it."

TRYING to dodge my colleagues while the football was on yesterday afternoon, but one of them finds me and declares: "My girlfriend goes on and on about the fillings of duvets and pillows." I know there is more to come, so I stand there until he adds: "So I said to her, 'I've told you before, don't talk down to me'."

A DAFT yarn from the bad weather where a Partick reader tells us about a huge puddle forming outside a pub in Ireland, and an auld fella standing beside it holding a stick with a string on the end, jiggling it up and down in the water.

A passing tourist asked what he was doing, and when the auld yin said "Fishing." The tourist took pity on him and invited him into the pub for a whiskey. Inside he couldn't stop himself from asking the old man: "How many have you caught."

"You're the eighth," he replied.

TOO late, a colleague catches our eye and comes over to tell us: "My wife is leaving me because she says I'm obsessed by quizzes. Is she a) Overreacting b) Unfair or c) Irritating?"

AAH, the Paisley banter. Robin Gilmour was listening to Radio 4 where there was a discussion on where might be chosen to be

UK City of Culture in 2021, with Paisley already putting in a bid. A BBC reporter was sent to gauge the mood of the locals and he was heard asking an older gentleman: "Excuse me Sir, what do you think of the idea that Paisley is being proposed as the City of Culture for 2021?"

"You're having a laugh!" the gent replied, and continued on his way.

OUR mention of haunted houses reminds Kate Woods: "A friend of mine, brought up in a Glasgow scheme, married into a very posh Edinburgh family. One evening she and her mother-in-law were discussing haunted houses and she told her mother-in-law that her sister was convinced her house was haunted. Her mother-in-law asked, in a cut-crystal accent, and in total disbelief, 'A ghost, Jennifer? In a council house?'"

A COLLEAGUE spots me and races over to impart his controversial wisdom: "They say Rome wasn't built in a day. The jury's out on Motherwell, though."

KINGSTON Council in London is using a poster of a chap, em, micturating in his fireplace, with the headline "You wouldn't do this at home" in a bid to stop the anti-social activity of urinating in the street. The poster brings back memories for Jack Irvine, chairman of Media House International, of his days as a young reporter. Says Jack: "I had to visit a couple in the notorious Ferguslie Park area of Paisley. The wife asked if I wanted a cup of tea. When I said yes she reached over to the kitchen sink and plucked a cup from the large pile of dirty dishes. To be fair, she rinsed it.

"Just at that her gangster husband emerged from his bedroom - it was early afternoon - wearing only a rather grubby vest, walked up to the sink, and proceeded to urinate therein.

"I got the story but declined the tea."

A BEARSDEN reader passes on her friend's comment after they met up for a cup of coffee. Her friend sank into her chair in the cafe and announced: "Based on the amount of laundry I did today I have to assume there are people living in my house that I haven't met yet."

THIS week is the 75th anniversary of the Clydebank Blitz. Not much to smile about in that horrendous time, but we do feel the need to recall the classic Clydebank Blitz tale of the couple leaving their top-floor tenement flat when the air raid siren sounded. At the bottom of the stairs the wife stopped and declared: "I'll need to go back up. Ahve left ma teeth."

Disabusing her, hubby replied: "It's bombs they're droppin' – no' aipples."

WE asked for your removal men stories, and Dr John Macpherson in Troon tells us: "My wife and I were in temporary hospital accommodation and had stored our furniture and belongings in a nearby lock-up garage. When we showed the removal man the packed contents of the garage he said, 'A bit small - but it will be nice when you get the carpets in'."

WE asked about removals, and Eunan Coll tells us: "A friend of mine in Glasgow's South Side was pottering about in his front garden one afternoon when he spotted a large removal lorry outside the house four doors down. There was a woman issuing instructions to the removal driver and when the lorry moved off my friend toddled along, stuck out his hand and said, 'Welcome to the Avenue. I hope you will be happy here, and if you have any problems I live just four doors along.' 'Thanks very much', she replied, 'but my family are just leaving - we've been living here for the past 11 years'."

YES, we all make mistakes, but we did like the correction issued by American news agency AP that stated: "This story has been corrected to show that the cardinal's name is Reinhard Marx, not Karl."

WISE words from a reader who tells us: "When I was young I used to think it would be exciting if you had the power to read other people's minds. Now that I've been on Facebook and Twitter for a while, I think I'm over it."

A BEARSDEN reader contacts us to ask: "Do you think it's called a remote because those are the odds of you finding it when you want to change the channel?"

TODAY'S piece of whimsy comes from a reader who tells us: "Whenever I see someone with their jumper tied round their waist I always imagine that they are being hugged by a short ghost."

A COLLEAGUE looks quite proud of himself as he wanders over and declares: "Fee, Fi, Fo, Fum ... I smell the conclusion of a game of Scrabble."

SPRING is finally arriving in Scotland. A Lenzie reader admits to us: "I was first in my street to cut the grass at the weekend, and now all the other husbands are looking at me as if I was the lad in school who reminded teacher she hadn't given us any homework."

A READER emails with advice: "Lost your keys? Why not try looking in the same two places 16 times while getting increasingly angry."

22
Sport

Of course it wouldn't be Scotland without a tale or two about football, although we managed to squeeze in one or two other sports as well.

THE football season has begun and a sports reporter tells us he was challenged by an over-enthusiastic steward to prove he was a member of the press at a sparsely-attended game last week. He tells us: "It reminds me of *The Herald's* late, great sports writer Ian 'Dan' Archer who was similarly stopped at a ground and asked to prove who he was. Dan simply leaned towards the steward and replied: 'Do you honestly think I would want to be here if I wasn't being paid to do so?'"

CANNOT believe it is all of 30 years this week since that great Celtic and Scotland manager Jock Stein died. We remember current Scotland manager Gordon Strachan talking about his playing career when Jock substituted him during a Scotland game against France. Sitting for the remainder of the game in the dug-out, Gordon remarked to a fellow player: "What a poor game this is."

Jock heard him and replied: "Aye, but it's got a lot better since you came off."

THE Great Scottish Run took to the streets of Glasgow yesterday with a half-marathon and a 10k race attracting thousands. Scott Agnew tells us he heard one spectator tell the child with her: "There's yer da. Give him a clap - for wance he's shifted the length o' hisell."

A READER sees the BT Sport headline "Olympic champion Mo Farah likely to skip World Indoor Championships" and he thinks to himself: "Oh come on Mo, that's just showing off."

WE asked for your supporters' bus stories and Eric Simpson in Dalgety Bay encompasses trains as well and says: "I was with a crowd of Buckie Thistle supporters travelling in a special train to Huntly for a cup-tie.

"As kick-off neared, the train was still some distance away. An irate fan opened the window and bawled, 'It's a fitba match we're gaan tae, nae a funeral!' "His *cri de coeur* made no difference and we still arrived late. As the crowd hastened towards the station exit, a callow youth endeavoured to inspect each ticket. There was an angry roar, and a charge that swept the hapless ticket collector aside.

"Sadly, I can't remember the score."

SCOTTISH celebrities have contributed to the new book, *My Scotland: By Its Famous Sons and Daughters*, released this week for charity. In it impersonator Rory Bremner talks about playing golf at St Andrews where he hit the ball into a huge bush. His impassive caddy remarked: "Ye could wrap that up in bacon, sir, and Lassie'd no find it."

NOT really unexpected news - the so-called businessman who briefly owned Rangers, Craig Whyte, has been declared bankrupt. A reader asks: "Will he just take a tip from American billionaire Donald Trump, call himself The Craig, and carry on as if nothing has happened?"

AT the recent biennial dinner of the Lothians Golf Association, says Bill Lothian, ex-pro David Huish looked back at a tournament career that included leading the Open at the halfway stage in 1975.

"I should have won that Open but for a disgraceful rules decision by the R&A," he said, causing the audience to ponder what awful transgression had occurred. "Back in 1892," Huish went on, "they decided to change from a 36-hole to a 72-hole competition."

ADAM Powley and Robert Gillan have written the book Shankly's Village about the now disappeared Ayrshire mining village Glenbuck, which produced so many great football players. They explain that the Glenbuck players went on to help develop other clubs such as nearby Kilmarnock, and tell the tale: "Kilmarnock keeper Bob Rankin, in one game as darkness descended, hit upon the idea of moving away from his goal to stand between the post and the touchline, loudly shouting at his defenders.

"The opposition, unable to see the goal in the dark, shot in the direction Rankin's shouts were coming from, sending the ball harmlessly away from the Kilmarnock goal." Genius.

WE mentioned free entry to Firhill on Saturday for students who apply in advance. A Thistle fan reminds us to warn them: "Students - free entry to Firhill, but do remember. It's a break-fast-time kick-off. 3pm."

MY afternoon nap in the office is disturbed by stout-hearted gentlemen making the Scottish Junior Cup draw in the *Evening Times* corral. Ayrshire rivals Auchinleck Talbot and Cumnock were drawn together, and we remember it was only a few years ago that police horses were summoned on to the park to restore order in the same fixture. However the story we liked was when the two teams played at Cumnock, and an Auchinleck winger kept on being hit by cigarette butts flicked by home fans. His answer was to pick up one of the lit fags, puff on it briefly, then complain loudly about the quality of Cumnock tobacco.

CELTIC fans will welcome the news that the club are to unveil a statue to Lisbon Lion captain Billy McNeill next month before their game against Motherwell. We always liked the story about Billy when he was Celtic manager and asked midfielder Peter Grant before a crucial Old Firm game to heavily mark Graeme Souness, even if it meant the risk of fouling the Rangers star. He then told the crestfallen Peter: "Don't worry about being sent off. They'll miss him more than we'll miss you."

THE chairman of the Scottish Referees' Association says it might consider allowing referees to give interviews after matches to explain decisions. It reminds reader Hugh Brennan: "Pity they don't have the communication skills of the late Tom 'Tiny' Wharton. Tom liked to tell the story of an Old Firm match when he disallowed a 'goal' for Rangers. As he ran backwards towards the centre circle a voice behind him from Jim Baxter exclaimed, 'You're a blind b*****d referee'. 'What did you say, Mr Baxter?' asked Tiny. Baxter replied, 'Oh, Christ, don't tell me you're deaf as well!'"

OUR mention of Ayrshire junior football reminds Alan Woodison of his first visit to Auchinleck Talbot as a raw junior reporter with the Cumnock Chronicle in the seventies. He confesses he knew nothing about football and even less about the wily ways of the juniors who were allowed, at the start of the season, to field trialists without naming them.

His ignorance of such matters was abundantly clear when, sensing a good news story from the Talbot teamsheet, asked if the back three - Newman, Newman and Newman - were brothers.

WELL done to Andy Murray making the final of the Australian Open. Adam Kay had a new take on an old debate by remarking: "Isn't it weird that when Djokovic wins a match he's Serbian, but when he loses he's Balkan?"

SAD to see that former Scotland star Duncan Ferguson, who played for Rangers and Everton, has been declared bankrupt. We remember when big Dunc took on two burglars, putting one in hospital. An alarm company worker told us he fitted an alarm at Dunc's converted barn house after the burglary. He said: "I told them that the number for the alarm was 1111 – you could then reset it to a number of your choice. I left him my number to phone if there were any problems, and I had only been gone five minutes when he phoned to ask: 'What was that number again?'"

SOMEHOW we stumbled into stories about Rangers legend John Greig, and Paul O'Sullivan reminds us: "Was there not an Old Firm game where John Greig tackled Bobby Lennox and Lennox was stretchered off with a broken leg? On Scotsport Bobby was interviewed at the hospital with his leg in plaster by Archie McPherson who asked him: 'When did you realise your leg was broken?' Bobby replied: 'When I saw John Greig running towards me.'"

JOHN Gilligan recalls the tale of the late Tom "Tiny" Wharton: "Scotland legend Wee Davie Wilson tells of the time he was caught ever so slightly by a tackle from the erudite John Lambie. Down went Davie. 'Penalty' said Tiny. 'That was never a ******* penalty!' screamed John. 'I'm afraid it is Mr Lambie. And if you don't believe me, read the *Sunday Post* in the morning,' said Tiny."

WE somehow began tackling the stories of legendary referee "Tiny" Wharton, and an Edinburgh reader recalls the Hearts winger Johnny Hamilton in the 1960s who had false teeth, which he left in the dressing room while playing. In one particular game Johnny was booked early on, then involved in a second-half altercation and was called over by Tiny. Says our reader: "Tiny merely pointed towards the tunnel and told him: 'The time has come, Mr Hamilton, for you to rejoin your teeth'."

AND Lisbon Lion Bertie Auld recalled, when he played for Birmingham City against Espanyol, his English teammates urged him to say something nice to the referee, Tiny Wharton, before the game. So Bertie said: "Well how about that, you and me the only Scots on the pitch in a big European tie."

Tiny said nothing, but in the second half he went over to

Bertie after a wild challenge and told him: "Remember when you said there would be two Scots on the pitch tonight? Now there's only going to be one. Off you go."

WE did blow time on the late referee Tom "Tiny" Wharton stories but an extra-time yarn comes from a number of readers who cannot agree whether it was Celtic's Jimmy Johnstone or Rangers' Tommy McLean who ran beside Tiny - who was in fact six feet four, muttering: "It's no' fair." Tiny asked the player what was not fair.

"That I have to pay the same as you for a suit," was the diminutive winger's reply.

AND our mention of Bertie Auld reminds John Henderson: "I liked the Bertie Auld story on tunnel psychology before the kick-off. He said he was waiting in the tunnel at an Old Firm match in the late 1960s and John Greig tried to psych out the Celtic team by asking what their win bonus was for the match. Bertie told him the Celtic bonus was £5 and Greig told him proudly that the Rangers players were on £10. 'Ah,' replied Bertie, 'but ours is guaranteed'."

THE joy of Premier League Darts comes to Glasgow's Hydro arena next month. Curiously darts was once banned in Glasgow pubs about 50 years ago as the council said it encouraged gambling and violence. A keen darts fan at the time asked a Glasgow bailie why dominoes, which also encouraged gambling, wasn't similarly banned. "Have you ever heard of anyone being stabbed with a domino?" the bailie memorably replied.

EXTRA time on referee Tom "Tiny" Wharton stories as Bryce Drummond recalls: "A junior football ref was at a seminar run by Tiny and asked if he arrived at a match, say in darkest Ayrshire, and a player bad-mouthed him and his refereeing skills before kick-off, did he have to let him play? 'Oh yes indeed,' replied Tiny. 'But not for long.'"

OUR story about the late Sam Galbraith not recognising actress Julie Christie reminds Jimmy Nimmo in Ayr: "At an Eagle Star "important client" fishing outing to a Tayside estate they owned, an aristocratic guest failed to recognise Nick Faldo or even hear his name correctly and asked, 'Well, what is it you do for a living, Mick? Nick merely replied, 'I play golf for a living'.

"At dinner that night after the fishing his lordship loudly announced, 'Well Mick, I do hope you are better at golf than you are at fishing, or it will be the poor-house for you, my lad!'"

THE *Herald* sports pages described this week's Inverness v Hearts goalless draw as "dire". We think the official social media feed of the Inverness club subtly agreed with my colleague. Halfway through the second half of the game, while giving a live commentary on the action, the club spokesman put on Twitter: "Just noticed that the press box windows could do with a wash."

IT'S all getting a bit exciting in the football this weekend, as teams try to avoid relegation while others try to achieve a top-six finish in the Scottish Premier League. An Inverness Caledonian Thistle fan declared on social media after doing a fair amount of arithmetic: "If Inverness beat Dundee United and Hearts, Hamilton beat Dundee and Ross County, and Partick Thistle draw, then we have a top-six finish." An unimpressed Jags fan, Colin Quinn, replied: "If Partick Thistle go undefeated for the next two seasons, they'll win the Champions League."

MEANWHILE former Liverpool manager Brendan Rodgers is favourite to become the new Celtic manager. We turn to social media for confirmation where Oldfirmfacts explains on Twitter: "Looks like the Celtic manager rumours are true. Just saw Brendan Rodgers in Sainsburys offering £32 plus a 10% sell-on clause for a Twix."

THE other big telly event at the weekend for many was the exciting Falkirk v Hibs play-off game, which Falkirk won with a goal in the last minute of injury time. One viewer said: "That's me deep in the wife's bad books. Her cat was on my lap when that last-minute Falkirk goal went in. Haven't seen it since."

And Ian Smith was perhaps just a tad harsh when he commented: "Falkirk fans celebrating like they've forgotten that they live in Falkirk."

BIT of a stushie over Muirfield not allowing lady members at its golf club. We liked the reaction of Stirling-born professional golfer Heather MacRae who commented: "The first time I played Muirfield I had to sit outside after the game as I wasn't allowed in. I sat and watched a member go in with his dog!"

FOOTBALL followers in Glasgow were getting aerated yesterday about Rangers signing controversial player Joey Barton. Celtic fans tried to deflate the optimism of Gers supporters by claiming Joey was a Celtic supporter in his youth. So we like the response of Rangers fan Chris Shuttleworth who declared: "Doesn't make a difference if Joey Barton is a 'Celtic fan'. We've signed him to play midfield, not run a supporters' club's away buses."

GERRY Burke was at Loch Fyne where he got chatting to a father and son fishing, new to the sport, who had the very best of expensive kit. They were fishing for mackerel.

Says Gerry: "I explained that hairy mussels off the shore were a good bait. 'Oh, I got something right then,' said the father. He had mussels in white wine sauce he had bought in the very expensive deli. Needless to say, had we mackerel we would have been delighted to swap."

RANGERS and Celtic fans are still taunting each other over who had the best signing this week - Celtic with new manager Brendan Rodgers or Rangers with midfielder Joey Barton. We hear of one Celtic fan who asked the Rangers fan in his office: "Did you see Brendan had 10,000 fans turn up to greet him at Celtic Park? How come so few Rangers fans turned up to see Joey?" "Because Rangers fans are at their work," he replied.

STILL great weather yesterday in the west of Scotland. Robin Gilmour was down at an Ayrshire golf club on the coast where the weather was clear enough to see across to Arran. A baffled American tourist who was playing the course exclaimed: "That island over there definitely wasn't there the last time I played here."

Says Robin: "This sunny weather with no wind or rain just confuses everyone."

WE pass on an interview with former Manchester United player Diego Forlan on a pre-season tour of America where there was a tennis court where they were staying, and he challenged star striker Ruud van Nistelrooy to a game. He added that only manager Sir Alex Ferguson knew Diego had been a junior tennis star before turning to football.

When asked what Sir Alex did, he said: "He was betting money on me."

OUR story about Muhammad Ali boxing in Paisley reminds Donald Cowan on Arran, who was a police constable at the time: "At the exhibition given in Paisley Ice Rink by Ali (Cassius Clay then), I and another constable who had a broken nose caused by a rugby accident, were escorting Cassius back to his dressing room. Cassius looked at the other constable, with his damaged nose, and asked: 'Are you a fighting man?'"

SOME engrossing games in Euro 2016, although there are still fears about crowd trouble. A Bridge of Weir reader emails us: "Over the weekend, hundreds of Polish fans arrived in Marseilles for Tuesday's game against Ukraine.

"Already there are reports that hundreds of cars have been washed and valeted, 90 boilers repaired and dozens of homes completely redecorated."

And a confused Martin McGeehan in Gourock asks: "If England face Northern Ireland at any stage, will 'God Save the Queen' be played twice? And if so, how will the English fans know when to boo?"

THERE was one Scotsman at least at Euro 2016 – controversial referee Willie Collum, who was in charge of the France v Albania game, and most of his critics had to grudgingly admit he had a reasonable match. Many Scots had bet on at least one player being sent off due to Willie's record in Scotland, but it was not to be.

After the game, former Dundee United player Ryan McGowan, who played for his native Australia, recalled: "Willie Collum at the Euros! During one game I was in I said to him: 'FFS

Willie! I can't believe you referee Champions League games. His reply: 'I can't believe you played in the World Cup'. Touché Willie, touché."

WE tried to think of a Scottish connection to Iceland giving England a right doing, when Eric Scott over in Bondi told us: "Great performance by that Scottish Icelander, Gaunyer Selson."

Someone also sent our friends south of the Border the pithy message: "Dear England. It's rubbish being out of Europe when you don't want to be. Your pals, Scotland."

But before we get too complacent, a reader in Cardiff passes on: "An Englishman, an Irishman and a Scotsman walk into a pub - to watch Wales play in the quarter-finals of Euro 2016."

AS Euro 2016 continues, there is still much debate about England's inability to score against Slovakia. Says Matt Vallance: "Just seen a cracking tweet about the England game, 'The last time the English were this bad at putting crosses into the box - we ended up with a Tory government'."

LOTS of runners out on the streets these days. A keep-fit fanatic tells us he was running along the Switchback at Bearsden when he suddenly, due to a bug, desperately needed to go to the loo, and in desperation ran into a small patch of trees where he had to quickly squat down. Unfortunately, he was joined by an inquisitive Labrador and, on hearing a woman shouting for her dog, he quickly jumped up and ran behind a tree to adjust his attire.

When he casually walked back out, he saw the woman with a plastic bag in her hand approaching the mess he had made and scolding her dog: "What have you been eating?"

WITH the football season beginning, Rangers fans have been reminiscing on a fans' chat-room about supporters' buses.

Said one: "On the old George's Cross bus to Kilmarnock, in agony for the loo as the traffic slowed down in Killie. Off the bus, ran into a restaurant, ran back out after a wee, caught up with another support-

ers' bus to get to the game. After the game caught a third bus back to Glasgow because I had lost all track of the guys, and no idea where they parked." He added, perhaps unnecessarily: "Cut down on the pints of heavy after that."

LOTS of middle-aged men in Glasgow buying top-of-the-range cycles to go out on the roads at the weekend. A reader heard one such cyclist declare: "My biggest fear is that if I died, my wife would sell my bicycles for what I told her they cost."

CHEEKY betting company Paddy Power is now taking wagers on the Olympics at Rio. They have announced in their advertisement that they will give the money back to anyone betting on a British competitor to win if they then come second to a Russian. The offer's headline is "Urine luck!"

THE wildest news - no, not the ostrich - was claims that Rangers were about to sign striker Robin van Persie.

Rangers fans were, of course, excited. Celtic fans, however, were quick to rubbish it. As one put it: "Van Persie? With their credit rating, Rangers couldn't even get van hire."

INTRIGUING Euro game between Germany and Italy at the weekend. A reader was watching it in a Glasgow pub where a punter declared after Italy's goal: "Do you know, that's nearly 10 hours since Germany last conceded a goal in a major tournament."

"That's nothing," replied someone further up the bar. "It's 18 years since Scotland conceded a goal in a major tournament."